Three Incredible Weeks with Meher Baba

September 11th to September 30th, 1954

Part I. The Diary
By Charles Purdom and Malcolm Schloss

Part II. Facets of the Diamond
By Baba's Western Devotees

Sheriar Press

Contents

Three Incredible Weeks
with Meher Baba

II. The Facets of the Diamond

Foreword

The life of Meher Baba is an extraordinary one, in the real sense that it is not the life of an ordinary man but one whose consciousness and destiny are beyond our own. As Meher Baba dictated in His message of September 7th, 1953, He was "not a *sadhu*, not a saint, not a *yogi*, not a *Mahaparusha*, not a *wali*," but the "Highest of the High" — the Avatar, a man fully conscious of God yet fully living the life of man.

What is such a life like?

It is a life of continual service to mankind — to the individual who needs His help, worldly or spiritual, and to the mass of humanity which needs His spiritual example and impetus at a critical turn in history. The lives of such God-men are often cryptically recorded, difficult to follow, subject to many religious and psychological interpretations. The life of Avatar Meher Baba is no exception, but it has one advantage over the lives of past Avatars — it has been more fully and accurately recorded in print and photo media.

Meher Baba's life (1894-1969) alternated between intense activity and deep seclusion, journey and rest. There was His early training of male and female disciples; His constant aid to the poor, ill and destitute, and the depressed classes of India. There was His work with spiritually advanced children; His inner spiritual work with the God-intoxicated and God-mad *masts* (over 7,000 in a few years) and with the saints, *sadhus* and *walis* of His time. There were His many lightning-like journeys to the West and Mideast; there was His dictation of innumerable letters, cables, messages and discourses. Almost all these activities took place during His self-imposed vow of Silence: from July 10, 1925, Meher Baba communicated only by means of an alphabet board, until October 7th, 1954, when He gave up the board for His unique hand-gesture language. This Silence, and its promised breaking, were a striking feature of the God-man's life. As we see in the Buddha's renunciation, the exile of Rama, the suffering of Christ, the Avatar always puts Himself under the yoke of some discipline, not for His own gain (He strives not for the Goal, He *is* the Goal), but for the benefit of mankind.

The period which this book covers is very short but very intense: an East-West gathering of His male followers, over 16 years old, for a three-week *satsang* or stay with the Master, from September 11th to September 30th, 1954. In it are blended many things: the personal loving contact with each devotee and His contact with the masses; the humorous down-to-earth companionship and the august "Final Declaration;" the wisdom teachings and the playful games; the quiet meditations and the active trips and recreations. Meher Baba was always universal in approach, and like all Avatars, followed His own whims and not the religious stereotypes of the past.

Through the eyes of the participants, we can follow the script of these truly incredible three weeks and vicariously enjoy the company of an incredible spiritual being — a living Perfect One.

This unique diary, written at Baba's request, is the combined work of Charles Purdom, noted writer, former editor of *Everyman* Magazine, and author of the *God-Man*, an autobiography of Meher Baba; and of Malcolm Schloss, noted mystical poet, who passed away on his return from India on October 7th, on the very day Baba gave up His alphabet board, which Baba termed "very fortunate." The diary and "Facets of the Diamond," the reminiscences of other Westerners who attended, were printed in two issues of the *Awakener* magazine, 1954-5. We are very pleased to reprint this account, with some additional material, in cooperation with Sheriar Press.

—Filis Frederick
Editor
The Awakener Magazine

The Diary

By Charles Purdom and Malcolm Schloss

Outside the tomb on Meherabad hill: Meher Baba with Westerners attending Three Incredible Weeks.

Introduction

Between September 7th and September 10th, 1954, twenty* Western men, disciples and devotees of the Perfect Master, Meher Baba, arrived in Bombay. They came from Europe, Australia and America. Their ages ranged from 25 to 80. Their occupations varied widely. There were several literary men; a petroleum chemist; an interior decorator; an importer and exporter; a postal officer; a luggage instructor; a buyer for an antique shop in London; a town planner; an economist. On September 11th we set out for Ahmednagar in two buses which had been chartered by Meherji Karkaria and Nariman Dadachanji; two of Baba's intimate disciples from Bombay, who also accompanied the Western group to Ahmednagar. There we met two more devotees from England who had arrived earlier.

It had been planned for the Western visitors to stay in the houses of a number of Baba's disciples in Ahmednagar, but Baba finally concluded that it would be better and easier for them and for Him to have them all together under one roof. So He decided on an unprecedented move. Upon the hill at Meherabad was the large two-story stone house which had served for years as a retreat for Baba's secluded women disciples. Baba had been the only man to set foot in the retreat, with the exception of Dr. Nilkanth, a Hindu disciple, who, being a physician, was called for consultation when needed. Baba decided that the retreat should now be used for the Western men, who were accordingly conducted there late in the evening of September 11th.

The upper story had been converted into a dormitory, where 20 iron beds, with springs, mattresses, sheets, pillows, blankets and mosquito nets, were ranged along the sides of the large room. (The Eastern men in the

*21, counting Zandor Markey who came for the Last Meeting.

ashram below slept on bedding-rolls stretched out on the stone floor). There were several dressing tables and a number of wardrobes for clothing. A bath towel and a face towel were provided for each visitor. In addition to the dormitory there were two rooms on the ground floor, with accommodations for several men. Also on the ground floor was a large community lounge.

Back of the house was a refectory with three tables stretched lengthwise, end to end, under a corrugated iron roof. Here the meals were served by three men waiters. A little beyond were the kitchens, where a cook and two or more assistants functioned; five bathrooms, three washstands with soap and running cold water and mirrors for shaving; and five toilets. Early in the morning buckets half-full of steaming hot water were brought by several men servants to the bathroom as required, where they were mixed with running cold water from taps on the wall. Soap and a large cup for dipping and pouring stood on a shelf above.

The meals were nourishing, varied, and delicious. For breakfast there was fruit, cereal, eggs, toast, butter, marmalade, cheese, milk, tea, coffee. The luncheons and dinners were equally sumptuous. Our clothes were laundered, pressed or cleaned as it became necessary. Our outgoing mail was posted for us and our incoming mail was delivered to us. Medicines were supplied for those who needed them.

In charge of all these arrangements were Sarosh Irani and his charming wife Viloo. Sarosh provided everything, from cigarettes to station wagons, and assisted by his most efficient secretary, Savak Damania, attended to all our necessary government papers and other bureaucratic red tape. Viloo was busy from early morning until late at night, planning our menus, securing supplies, supervising the preparation and the cooking of the food. In all this she was ably assisted by Savak Kotwal, who stayed at the retreat with us and saw that everything ran smoothly.

Savak rose at 4 a.m., awakened the servants at 4:30, and retired after we did, which was usually by 10:30 p.m., although some of us were occasionally working until midnight. The sanitary arrangements and our general health were in charge of Dr. Donkin, who came up every morning with sprays of various kinds and insecticides and other necessary supplies.

Nothing that could reasonably contribute to our comfort or well-being was overlooked. Baba proved Himself to be a perfect host as well as a Perfect Master.

What follows is a day-by-day account of what happened externally, from the morning of September 12th to the evening of September 30th, when we left Meherabad for Bombay and our journey home. Actually, what happened externally was only important as a manifestation of the loving care with which we were treated by Baba on down to the humblest of the servants. Even the teaching that Baba gave us, on which He spent hours of careful exposition, was relatively unimportant. Actually, it was a diversion intended to satisfy our intellects while Baba worked on the deeper levels of our consciousness. As Baba said, during a relatively small *darshan* program which He gave on the afternoon of September 26th, to take care of some 2,500* people who had missed the large mass *darshan* of the 12th, "No explanations or discourses can compare with this personal contact." And we, for some reason known only to Baba, were privileged to live in intimate association with Him for three wonderful weeks!

*Darwin Shaw gives 8,000 as the figure

Meher Baba's Last Mass Darshan
Sunday, September 12

In response to Meher Baba's invitation to attend His important meetings at Meherabad in September, 1954, we eighteen* men disciples and devotees of Baba from Europe, Australia and America arrived at Meherabad late in the evening of September 11th.

Arising early in the morning of the 12th, we were transported shortly after eight o'clock to Wadia Park in Ahmednagar, where Baba's Last Mass Darshan was to be held. On our arrival at the gaily decorated park, we were led to the huge *pandal*, or tent without sides, which had been erected especially for the occasion. Some 10,000 people had already arrived, and were seated both in the *pandal* and beside it, the men on one side, the women on the other, as is the custom in India. Sarosh Irani, who was elected Mayor of Ahmednagar while he was in the United States with Baba in 1952, greeted us warmly and conducted us to the platform at the end of the tent where Baba was to be seated during the *darshan*, introducing us to Swami Sahajanand Bharathi, the leader of the Congress Party from the Ahmednagar District; Mr. P.R. Kanawade, Member of Parliament from the Ahmednagar District, and Mr. K.G. Pardeshi, the present Mayor of Ahmednagar, all of whom were later to make addresses in honor of Baba. Also on the platform were fourteen women disciples of Baba's second Master, Upasni Maharaj, who had come from Sakori, led by Upasni's favorite disciple, Godavri Mai, who is now in charge of His ashram there; the Jessawalla and the Deshmukh families from Nagpur; several of Baba's devotees from Southern India; and several of Baba's Mandali.

Precisely at nine o'clock Baba arrived. Giving the impression of infinite, yet completely controlled power, He strode to the platform, spelled out on His alphabet-board,

*Two arrived later

"Not as man to man, but as God to God, I bow down to you, so as to save you the trouble of bowing down to Me."

Descending the steps to the edge of the platform while this announcement was being broadcast over a public address system in English and Marathi, Baba prostrated Himself before the assembled multitude.

Mounting the steps again, He spelled out on His board, "To make you all share My feeling of being one with you and one of you, I sit down beside you." While this was being broadcast, Baba descended from the platform and sat first among the men, and then among the women.

"To make you all share My feeling of being one with you and one of you, I sit down beside you."

Returning to the platform, He washed the feet of seven poor men, after which He gave to each a gift of 51 rupees, saying, "As each one of you is, in one way or another, an Incarnation of God, I feel happy to bow down to you and to lay at your feet this *Dev-Dakshana*." *Dev-Dakshana* is a gift offered to a Perfect Master or to a deity.

"As each one of you is, in some way or another, an Incarnation of God, I feel happy to bow down to you and to lay at your feet this Dev Dakshana.*"*

Baba then resumed His seat on the platform, and the following two messages by Him were broadcast in English and Marathi.

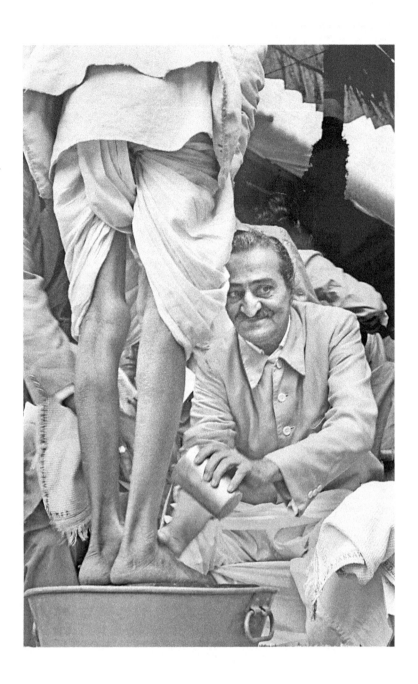

4 Three Incredible Weeks

Messages of Meher Baba

I

If you were to ask me why I do not speak, I would say I am not silent, and that I speak more eloquently through gestures and the alphabet board.

If you were to ask me why I do not talk, I would say, mostly for three reasons. Firstly, I feel that through you all I am talking eternally. Secondly, to relieve the boredom of talking incessantly through your forms, I keep silence in my personal physical form. And thirdly, because all talk in itself is idle talk. Lectures, messages, statements, discourses of any kind, spiritual or otherwise, imparted through utterances or writings, is just idle talk when not acted upon or lived up to.

If you were to ask when I will break my silence, I would say, when I feel like uttering the only real Word that was spoken in the beginningless beginning, as that Word alone is worth uttering. The time for the breaking of my outward silence to utter that Word, is very near.

When a person tells others "Be good", he conveys to his hearers the feeling that he is good and they are not. When he says "Be brave, honest and pure", he conveys to his hearers the feeling that the speaker himself is all that, while they are cowards, dishonest and unclean.

To love God in the most practical way is to love our fellow beings. If we feel for others in the same way as we feel for our own dear ones, we love God.

If instead of seeing faults in others we look within ourselves we are loving God.

If instead of robbing others to help ourselves, we rob ourselves to help others, we are loving God.

If we suffer in the suffering of others, and feel happy in the happiness of others, we are loving God.

If instead of worrying over our own misfortunes, we think of ourselves more fortunate than many, many others, we are loving God.

If we endure our lot with patience and contentment, accepting it as His Will, we are loving God.

If we understand and feel that the greatest act of devotion and worship to God is not to hurt or harm any of His beings, we are loving God.

To love God as He ought to be loved, we must live for God and die for God, knowing that the goal of all life is to love God, and find Him as our own Self.

II

When I say I am the Avatar, there are a few who feel happy, some who feel shocked, and many who hearing me claim this, would take me for a hypocrite, a fraud, a supreme egoist, or just mad. If I were to say every one of you is an Avatar, a few would be tickled, and many would consider it a blasphemy or a joke. The fact that God being One, Indivisible and equally in us all, we can be nought else but one, is too much for the duality-conscious mind to accept. Yet each of us is what the other is. I know I am the Avatar in every sense of the word, and that each one of you is an Avatar in one sense or the other.

It is an unalterable and universally recognised fact since time immemorial that God knows everything, God does everything, and that nothing happens but by the Will of God. Therefore it is God who makes me say I am the Avatar, and that each one of you is an Avatar. Again, it is He Who is tickled through some, and through others is shocked. It is God Who acts, and God Who reacts. It is He Who scoffs, and He Who responds. He is the Creator, the Producer, the Actor and the Audience in His own Divine Play.

Next, came seven speeches eulogizing Baba; the performance of *Arti* by six young women in light-blue saris, waving camphor lamps; *bhajans*, or devotional songs, by native musicians; and a repetition of the *Arti* by R.K. Gadekar, one of Baba's disciples from Poona.

Six nuns from Sakori sing bhajans *for Baba.*

Then came the main event of the program, the *darshan* and the giving of *prasad*, which means "a gift from God," to what seemed like an endless procession of men, women and children, flowing for eight hours past Baba, who had seated Himself on the lower edge of the platform, and who gave to each who passed a handful of sweetmeats, while they tried to touch His feet either with their heads or with their hands. The multitude, which had gathered early in the morning, was continually being augmented by new arrivals, even after Baba had left, with *kirtans* † being sung until ten o'clock at night, and by the time the program was concluded, 60,000 people had received their "gift from God."

"Come All Unto Me" — *entering the stage on September 12, 1954*

The swiftly flowing stream of humanity that wound past Baba was at first smooth and orderly in its rhythm, a graceful procession of women in colorful saris, lovingly presenting their children to their beloved Master.

† Devotional songs.

Towards noon the orderly flow of women and children was interrupted by a gigantic tidal wave of turbaned men, who, impatient for their turn, pressed forward on their side to the edge of the platform, in spite of all efforts by the Ahmednagar police and Baba's Mandali to restrain them. It seemed, for a few minutes, as if they would inundate Baba. The din was terrific, both on the floor and on the platform, where exhortations by Sarosh, Pardeshi and others for the men to return to their places were shouted into the microphone and broadcast throughout the huge *pandal*. Finally, Baba mounted His seat on the platform and motioned for them to go back, which they reluctantly did, and the stream flowed on again in swift but orderly fashion.

Baba gives out prasad *to the multitudes.*

As the procession continued, Baba would now and then pat some child on the cheek, some man or woman on the head, or recall some woman who had been pushed ahead before He could give her *prasad*. In the early afternoon His right hand grew so weary that He started giving out the sweets with His left. When some of His disciples asked Him to rest, He replied, "This is My rest." Every so often He would glance about the platform at us, sometimes smiling, sometimes gesticulating, as the occasion seemed to warrant.

The crowds would not eat until Avatar took His food.

At three o'clock He left the platform and was away for fifteen minutes at another part of the park, where 20,000 poor people who were being fed by Him, were seated, waiting for Him to begin their repast, which consisted of wheat grains with curry-sauce, served on large leaf plates. They would not think of eating until Baba first partook of their food.

Seated alongside of Baba on the edge of the platform all during the *darshan* was Gadge Maharaj, an elderly saint* who is highly respected throughout India. Every so often loving exchanges would take place between Baba and Gadge , and occasionally incidents would occur which seemed to amuse them highly. One woman, who evidently

Gadge Maharaj, a 6th plane saint, watches Baba give darshan, *September 12, 1954.*

believed in collecting as many blessings as possible while she could, having touched Baba's feet and received her "gift from God," tried also to touch Gadge's feet as she passed him. Gadge drew himself up in displeasure, but Baba smiled and Gadge softened.

*Baba said he was on the 6th plane.

One of the most extraordinary features of the program was the appearance on the platform, in the late afternoon, of those women disciples of Baba who had heretofore been in seclusion—their first appearance in public.

It was wonderful to see again many of Baba's closest disciples, whom we had met and come to love either on previous visits to India or when they accompanied Baba on His journeys to the West, and to meet for the first time some of His devotees from southern India, all of whom contributed considerably to that strange, but marvelous dissolving process which always takes place when one is with Baba.

The last glimpse we had of Baba as He left the park was one in which He was seated on the top of an automobile, bowing in every direction to crowds of people reluctant to let Him go. He had seated Himself first on the hood, giving *darshan* to late-comers, but the press grew too great, and He retreated to the top, and the car moved slowly out of the park with the Avatar in a distinctly novel position.

For all of us this last "Mass Darshan" of Baba will be a memorable event which will grow in significance as we grow in understanding. We are grateful to Baba for having made it possible for us to participate in it.

The *Times of India* reported the event as follows:

Sri Meher Baba Blesses 15,000 Followers

DAY-LONG CEREMONY HELD AT AHMEDNAGAR

Ahmednagar, September 12. Sri Meher Baba, the 61-year old Indian mystic who claims to be an 'avatar' of God, blessed a congregation of more than 15,000 of his followers, at a solemn ceremony, here today.

He said: "May the spark of my divine love implant in

your hearts a deep longing for the love of God."

The vast gathering, which included his disciples from America, England, Australia and Switzerland, swelled to more than 25,000 towards the evening.

The disciples listened in reverential silence to the message read out to them on the occasion of Meher Baba's public *darshan* to his followers in Ahmednagar for the first time in 25 years.

In the message, he enjoined on them: "Live not in ignorance. Do not waste your precious life-span in differentiating between, and judging your fellowmen, but learn to long for the love of God. Be pure and simple, and love all, because all are one."

Sri Meher Baba, who began his work of awakening the public at Ahmednagar 40 years ago, told his followers: "Spare no pains to help others. Seek no other reward than the gift of divine love."

Sri Meher Baba, whose mission is to change the world, has not uttered a word for the last 29 years and has written nothing except his signature in the last 27 years.

For conveying his thoughts and ideas, he uses a board on which the English alphabet is inscribed.

In his message today, he observed: "If you were to ask me when I will break my silence, I would say, it will be when I feel like uttering the only real word that was spoken in the beginning, as that word is worth uttering. The time for breaking my outward silence to utter that word is very near."

Sri Meher Baba normally lives in seclusion but he has travelled round the world three times. He has visited England and the continent ten times.

Among those present at the congregation today were 20 disciples of Meher Baba from abroad, including Mr. C.B. Purdom, British author and journalist, Mr. Malcolm Schloss, author and poet, and Mr. Frank S. Hendrick, American author, and Mr. Francis Brabazon, noted Australian poet, Shri Gadejai Maharaja, a spiritual leader with a considerable following in Maharashtra, was also present.

"Perfect Master"

On his arrival at Wadia Park where the ceremony which lasted from 9 a.m. to 5 p.m. was held, Sri Meher Baba prostrated before the congregation "not as man to man but God to God," so as to save them the trouble of bowing down to him.

A unique function, which formed an important part of the day-long ceremony, was the washing of the feet of seven poor octogenarians from all religions, by Meher Baba himself.

The ceremony began with a welcome speech by Mr. Sarosh K. Irani, chairman of the reception committee.

It was followed by the presentation of a civic address by the Ahmednagar municipality. Speeches in appreciation of Meher Baba's work of awakening the people to the unity of spiritual knowledge and love were made, among others by Swami Sahajanand Bharati, president of the Ahmednagar District Congress Committee, Mr. P.R. Kanavade, M.P., Mr. T.S. Bharade, M.L.A., and Mr. N.E. Navie, a former M.L.C.

There was a scramble when Meher Baba began distributing *prasad* to his devotees and followers.

This program continued for about five hours and terminated in the evening.

Sri Meher Baba has convened a meeting of his followers from all over the world on September 29 and 30 at Meherabad, in Ahmednagar, to explain to them his future program "before giving up his physical body."

———————◆———————

Kishansingh Pardeshi, President of the Ahmednagar Borough Municipality, gave a speech dedicated to "Shri Sadguru Meher Baba," — translated as follows:

Most Adorable Shri Meher Baba,

After a lapse of nearly 25 years, we, the people of the District of Ahmednagar, feel fortunate for being blessed by your august *darshan*. And, on behalf of all the inhabitants of this District, I have the great privilege to welcome you whole-heartedly on this occasion when you have blessed us all through your great love and your holy *darshan*.

Generation after generation, this land of ours — the abode of great Saints and Sages — has become blessed. This plateau of the Deccan has ever added to the glory of Bharat through its spiritual heritage and enlightening literature. Shri Dnyaneshwar of Newasa, Shri Changdev, Shri Sai Baba, Shri Upasani Maharaj of Kopargaon, Shri Mahipat of Rahuri, Shri Dinkar Swami of Pathardi, Shri Eknath of Shevgaon-Paithan, all of them hail from this District of Ahmednagar which is indeed blessed with spiritual atmosphere. And today, at this place, we feel that the treasure of all the accumulated spiritual heritage of this land of the Deccan has been laid bare before us through your public *darshan*.

Poona is the birthplace of Baba, and there Baba had his education. Again in Poona, at the time of his education, Baba had the first real *darshan* of Babajan. It was that close contact of Babajan that bestowed on Baba his Godhood. Shri Upasni Baba's close contact in the District of Ahmednagar made Baba realise his eternal Godhood. Since then, Baba's life became exceptionally supernatural; and since then, he began to reveal the Truth to all his devotees that it is possible for the soul to become one with the Over-Soul. All these years, Baba has stressed that the goal of life is to gain the grace of Perfect Masters, and to attain God-Realization.

It has become a common experience of many that though you have observed long years of silence, yet the spark of your Divine flame illumines the lives of many, and that too, just through mere *darshan* of your personality.

You are imparting the same spiritual knowledge which the Avatars of the past did impart; and all along, you have been emphasizing the same precept of the past that we should annihilate the bindings of the body-life, and realize the eternal "Oneness" in the "many."

Your only one message to the world is, "It is possible, through love, for man to become God; and when God becomes man, it is due to His love for His beings. Therefore, love God and you will find that your own self is nothing but God." Universal brotherhood, equality and love have been your three chief pointers to the world.

In order to awaken humanity, and to make mankind love God, you have not spared yourself to travel far and wide. You have paid frequent visits to Europe and America, and you have not left out any province in Bharat unvisited. Even while you had your headquarters at Ahmednagar, your help always reached the poor. Your work for the upliftment of the down-trodden untouchables, your work with the mad-men and the lepers, and all your different activities in many other spheres have set at work for the spiritual cause, both men and women of different nationalities; and of all castes and creeds all over the world; and you have filled the heart of many a family with joy and bliss through your personal contacts during your travels.

Your ever-peaceful, and your ever-smiling face, and your ever-bright eyes, full of spiritual radiance, are sufficient to fill any man with joy, and to make him pay homage at your feet on taking your *darshan*.

We, the people of Ahmednagar, feel grateful to you today for your grace that grants us this public *darshan* in the open, because we know that the Grace of the Perfect Master alone can emancipate all of us from the grip of our own ignorance.

> *"Grace of Masters is that Light*
> *which illumines the aspirants."*

It is only your love for the people of this District that has made you shower your grace upon us all today to grant this unique opportunity of the open *darshan* to the public.

On behalf of men and women of this District, I most humbly bow down while offering this address to you with all devotion.

Tuesday, September 14

After our day of rest yesterday, Baba arrived early in the morning of the 14th. The first thing He did was to embrace each of us in turn, after which He said that He would embrace us only today, otherwise His heart could not stand it. He then led us into the refectory and asked us to introduce ourselves, as there were some among us whom He was meeting outwardly for the first time. The group included Will Backett, Charles Purdom, and Fred Marks from England; Max Haefliger from Switzerland; Philippe DuPuis from France; Francis Brabazon, Bill LePage and John Ballantyne from Australia; Malcolm Schloss, John Bass, Darwin Shaw, Fred Winterfeldt, Frank Eaton, Lud Dimpfl, Joseph Harb, Fred Frey, Frank Hendricks, and Dana Field from America. After the introductions, He embraced us each again. Then He took up His alphabet board, which Eruch Jessawalla read for Him.

"Today I have three points that I wish to convey to you. The first is that I want you to be completely natural and absolutely frank. If the food does not agree with you, say so. If there is anything you don't like, say so. If your health is not good, say so. Sarosh and Viloo are in charge here. Tell them. If they can possibly change it, they will do so. If they can't change it, they will say 'yes' and that will be that.

"Don* is in charge of your health. If you have any difficulty of any kind, tell him. You must take care to keep yourself in good health, because the meetings on the 29th and 30th will be very important, and you must be in good shape to absorb everything that will be given.

"The second point is this: while you are here, from now until you leave, I want you to forget everything about Europe, America, and Australia, and think only of Baba and what you are experiencing here. If you only had a glimpse of what I really am, you would forget yourself completely and be conscious only of God. So, while you are here, try to forget Europe, America, and Australia, and be conscious only of what you experience here.

"The third point is this: these meetings on the 29th and 30th are very important. They will be the last meetings I will hold before I give up the body. There will be about a thousand present, from all over India and Pakistan—all workers for Baba. Everything I say will be spontaneous, and someone should take down every word, because there will be no prepared text, and it will be vitally important. I will tell you why I am here, what I have done, what I shall still do, and what will happen in seven hundred years. After all, you have all come a great distance to attend these meetings, and I want you to receive as much as you possibly can from them. Then, when they are over, I want you to go home as quickly and directly as possible, so that you can carry with you, still fresh, what you have received."

Baba then told us to get our sun-hats and come with Him. First He led us to the tomb, which He had built for Himself, which is located on the side of the hut in which He spent twelve months in seclusion years ago, taking only

*Dr. William Donkin

Entering the gates of Meherabad Ashram

coffee twice daily. Later He told us how, twice daily, a thermos bottle full of coffee had been ordered sent to Him from the ashram below. It was brought by a young boy, but each day, when the bottle arrived it was only half full. So Baba sent word for them to send Him a full bottle. Still, every day only half a bottle arrived. Finally, when the seclusion had ended, Baba sent for the woman in charge of the arrangements and asked her why she had sent Him only a half-bottle instead of a full one. She protested that she had always sent a full one. Baba then sent for the boy, who confessed that every day, half-way up the hill, he had grown tired, and had drunk half the coffee. Fortunately, Baba had not required even the half that was sent to Him. In fact, He was so strong, when He came out of seclusion, that 15 men of the Mandali, lined up one in back of another, could not push Baba one inch.

The inside of the tomb has been decorated with lovely murals by Helen Dahm of Switzerland. Then Baba led us outside and showed us the tombs of His mother and father, of Nonny Gayley, and of Nadia Tolstoy, stopping on the way to show us another room where He had shut Himself up many years ago for months, not seeing anyone, and only communicating with one of the Mandali through a small slit in the wall.

From here He led us down the hill at a brisk pace to the men's ashram, stopping once to ask Will Backett if He was walking too fast for him, and resuming at a slower pace even though Will replied in the negative. At the foot of the hill on the road into town, a bus full of natives had seen Baba descending the hill, and had stopped to pay their respects to Him; and other Hindus, men and women, from nearby, had also congregated to greet Him. As we entered the grounds of the ashram, a private bus drove up and fourteen of Upasni's women disciples from Sakori descended, and all of us entered the ashram, where the women prostrated themselves in turn before Baba, taking the dust of His feet. One of them was Godavri Mai, who, Baba said, was Upasni Maharaj's favorite disciple, and was now in charge of Upasni's ashram in Sakori, where thirty of Upasni's women disciples were now living. Second in command at Sakori was a gracious, elderly gray-haired woman, who was nicknamed "Jiji."

Baba, through Eruch, spoke to us and to them. One of the most important things He said was, "I am the One Reality."

Next Baba led us out to the little wooden hut, on legs, so small that one could not stand up straight inside of it, where He spent a number of months in seclusion in 1925, writing the account of His spiritual experience, which no one so far has seen. Adi said that this was not *God Speaks*, but a separate manuscript, which is now in a vault in a bank in Bombay.

Alongside this is Baba's *Dhuni*, or sacred fire. Vishnu,

one of Baba's Mandali told us of the drought in 1927, which was so severe that in desperation the villagers came to Baba imploring Him to send them rain; whereupon Baba lit the *Dhuni*, and by the time the villagers had returned to their village, which was close by, it was raining.

"They call it a miracle," said Baba, "but it was only a coincidence. I will perform only one miracle — when I speak the One Word — The Divine Word. That will really be a miracle."

Then He led us to another hut nearby, which we were told was the first into which He had retired in seclusion.

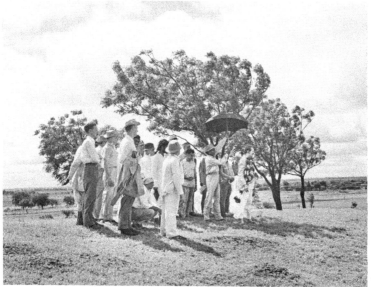

Man and God-Man

From here He led us back up the hill to our present quarters, motioning the women to take it in leisurely fashion. He stopped once on the way up and gathered the Western group about Him under a tree, throwing stones in oblique directions, which we were supposed to catch. As we continued up the hill, He bent down several times to pick up stones which He threw into the fields. On our arrival at the retreat, He took the women up the steps to see our quarters, then led them into the tomb, and to the room where He had rested in seclusion, after which He sent them back, advising them that He would come with us one day soon to Sakori.

Then He led the Western group into the lounge underneath our dormitory and told us, through Adi, that in the early days there was no door leading into this room—there was only the window which is now above the door — and that He used to let Himself in through the window, close it after Him, and stay there in seclusion for periods of time.

Then Baba moved over to the divan and began conversing with us, through the alphabet board of course, with Eruch and Adi translating. He stressed again the idea of our being perfectly natural and frank with Him.

"I am your Master," He said, "but I am also your friend. I am one of you and one with you."

Then He said that He would come to see us everyday between now and the 27th, unless the rains made the roads impassable, or unless He caught cold—"from one of you," He added jocularly. He would explain many things, He said, about the Spiritual Path, and Realization, and about His work, and what we could do to help Him in it, and He said that everything should be taken down, and then Purdom and Malcolm will get it into shape for publication. The rest could play, in the afternoon and evening, but Purdom and Malcolm would have to work. However, everyone was to be present every day between 9 and 12:30 while He was with us, so that each would receive as much as possible of what He had to give.

Then He said that Realization came, not through the intellect, but through the heart; from loving God and seeing God in and through everything. He spoke of the three kinds of conviction that both the Sufis and the

Vedantists define. The first is intellectual conviction, which is arrived at through reason and logic, as a result of which one is convinced that *God is*. The second is conviction by sight, and when one gets this, one *sees God* everywhere in everything, as clearly as one would see external objects, but with the inner eye. One is then free from all doubts, and experiences bliss. But the real conviction, He continued, is when one *becomes God*. Then one knows that only God exists, and that one and all are God. It is only when one gets this conviction that one really knows Baba.

"I am one with you on every level, but you know this only when the ego and intellect do not interfere. Then Baba appears as He is.

"I am what I am, whether the world bows down to Me, or whether it turns against Me; it does not matter. It is no one's fault.

"To know Baba is not a matter of eating Indian sweets. One has to die to oneself to know Me. It is not just a joke— this Love."

"Be happy, and forget everything except what you experience here. The meeting on the 29th and 30th will be unique, and it will be lasting in its effect. Until then, don't worry about anything; be cheerful, be honest, and look after your health. Then after the meeting is over I want you to go back directly to your destination and to take back intact the atmosphere of the meeting."

Baba then asked each of us to say something. Malcolm quoted one of the songs of Kabir, which ran, "Where is the need for words when Love has made drunken the heart?"

John Bass said, "I really don't know what to say. My mind is a blank."

"To be blank is an excellent thing," Baba replied.

Lud Dimpfl was next, and he said something about being tongue-tied, ending with, "And we sit here like a bundle of sticks!" Baba smiled, and replied, "Say 'I', not 'we.' "

Lud thought Baba was displeased with him, and said

something to that effect. He was greatly distressed. Baba reassured him.

"I love you, and I will never be displeased. Speak from your heart. If you hide what you feel, you will not be honest. I love you for being honest. I really love you. Say whatever you feel, but say 'I' not 'we.' Do you feel happy?"

Lud said he did, and Baba asked, what else was necessary?

Philippe told how deeply impressed he was with Baba's *darshan* on the 12th, and said something to the effect that it must have been a great strain on His body.

"Before I drop My body," Baba replied,"I will again go through violent attacks on the body. What has to happen will happen and I will gladly undergo all this for the sake of humanity. My only happiness lies in making people understand, not through the mind, but through experience, that God alone is the Beloved for Whom we exist. In the meeting, I will make this clear as never before, and any of you who are strong enough to carry out that message will do My work. It is only for this meeting that I have called you."

Joseph Harb said something to the effect that it was a privilege and a great joy to be here with Baba, and that he hoped he would be made a fit instrument to carry on the work.

Fred Winterfeldt said that when the heart is full, the mouth runs over; that he could scarcely believe that he was really here; and asked by what grace we could attain to the love which Baba described.

Frank Eaton spoke of being deeply impressed by the fellowship of Baba's disciples. Bill LePage and John Ballantyne said something that escaped recording, but it evoked from Baba a profound comment.

"One who wants nothing, gets everything," He said. "Nothing means nothing, and one who wants nothing, is never disappointed."

He asked Malcolm if this were not so, and received an

affirmative reply. Then He turned to Francis Brabazon, whose remarks also escaped recording, but in response Baba quoted a verse from Hafiz, which runs as follows:

"Do not ask for union with God, and do not bewail separation. Seek only the Will of the Beloved."

"Before I met My Beloved in union," Baba continued, "I lost everything...ego, mind, and lower consciousness; but thank God I did not lose My sense of humor. That is why I appear amongst you on your level."

Darwin Shaw said something that reminded Baba of an incident in New York in 1952, and asked Darwin if he remembered what had happened to Keith MacGaffey and himself in the Bronx Zoo.

Max Haefliger said, "I don't understand anything about you, but I like your people."

"That means you don't like Me?" asked Baba.

Max said something about liking Baba sometimes.

"So you like My people all the time," said Baba, "And you like Me sometimes."

Fred Frey said that he was up in a cloud; that Baba was just what he had expected; that he felt warmed inwardly by Baba's people; and that if he could bring Baba's love back to America it would make him most happy.

Will Backett said that his heart had echoed everything that had already been said, and that of course he was blissfully happy to be with Baba.

Charles Purdom said, "When you were speaking about the three types of conviction, I was reminded about what Jesus said in relation to seeing God—that only the pure in heart can see God. Would you explain that to us sometime?"

Baba promised that He would explain from tomorrow on. Then He turned again to Max. "Max, you don't like Me," He said. "Anyway, I like you all the same, all the time." Baba then repeated what He had said before, and elaborated on it.

"Before I met My Beloved in union — I lost everything, ego, mind, and lower consciousness, but thank God, I did not lose my sense of humor. That is why I appear amongst you like this, on your level. Yogis, saints, *sadgurus* in India you will usually find in meditation, with long beards. You would not be allowed in their presence with shoes on, or smoking, but with Me you can do all these things because I am one with you and one of you. From tomorrow I will work in order that this visit of yours will not be merely a picnic or a sightseeing trek."

Baba then turned to a description of the three types of lovers of God. "The first type," He said, "is the *mast*, who loves and knows only God. He loses all consciousness of self, of body, of the world. Whether it rains or shines, whether it is winter or summer, it is all the same to him. Only God exists for him. He is dead to himself and to the world. He exists no longer as an individual, for, after thus annihilating himself, he becomes one with God, the source of infinite love.

"The second type of lover is one who lives in the world, attends to all worldly duties one hundred per cent, yet all the time in his heart he knows that this is temporary, that only God exists, and he loves Him internally, without anyone knowing it.

"The third type, which is the highest, is very rare. Here the lover surrenders completely to the Christ, to the Avatar, to the God-Man. He lives, not for himself, but for the Master. This is the highest type of lover. Unless you have such love, just to criticize and judge will take you nowhere."

Baba then sent us to luncheon, and later joined us there, sitting first at one end of the table, and then at the other. He questioned each of us as to whether the food was to our liking, and received unanimous expressions of approbation. Then He took up His alphabet board.

"I wonder if you understand how fortunate you are to have Me with you in this way? Think of those people at the *darshan* on the 12th, who fought so to have a chance to touch My feet for just a fleeting second; who wanted so earnestly to receive *prasad*, which means 'a gift of God.'

"They are the ones who really love Me. The others, the social people, the political people, the intellectual people, they make their speeches and they leave the platform."

"In Andhra for fifteen days we had two or three *darshan* programs every day, with thousands of people coming from surrounding villages in bullock-carts and on foot. They would not understand your being here with Me this way. In India, they have traditions. As I told you before, yogis, saints and *sadgurus* are supposed to be sitting in silent meditation, with long beards. You could not make effective contact with them. Remember always that I am your Master, but that I am also your friend; that I am one with you, and one of you. Therefore you can be completely natural with Me, and tell Me frankly whatever is in your mind.

"When I am with *sadhus*, no one is more serious than I am. When I am with children, I play marbles with them. I am in all, and one with all. That is why I can automatically adapt Myself to all kinds of people, and meet them where they are."

Wednesday, September 15

Today was devoted entirely to private interviews with Baba of which it is of course impossible to say anything.

Thursday, September 16

We arose early this morning and left at 7a.m. for Pimpalgaon. On our arrival there, Baba led us first to the room where Kaikobad Dastur stayed, and introduced us all to him. For twelve years, he told us, Kaikobad has meditated in accordance with Baba's instructions. He repeats Baba's name a hundred thousand times a day. He observes regular watches every three hours, day and night, for meditation, and spends most of his time in seclusion. Baba had Kaikobad himself tell us how he sometimes sees stars, suns and moons coming out of himself. When the moon is in his head, everything is peaceful and he can enjoy the peace and bliss of the experience. When the sun is in his head, it is very difficult for him to maintain consciousness, and he often loses it.

Baba then led us to Kaka Baria's room and introduced him to those who had not yet met him, explaining that he was the Manager at Pimpalgaon, that his table was always cluttered with papers, because he had so much work to do, and that he had taken care of the garden when Baba and the girls were abroad in 1952. Baba said that it was Kaka who had named this place, "Meher Azad," and explained that *"Azad"* means free, whereas *"Abad"* means flourishing.

Baba then led us to His own room, and told us that in the Man-o-nash period* He worked very hard here for the whole world; that He had come out of the Man-o-nash period pale, thin and exhausted—as if something had been sucked out of Him. It was very rare for Him, he continued, to be in this condition. It had happened to Him once at Angarishi, on a mountain in the Central Provinces, where the *rishis* used to meditate, and where He had spent some time in a cave in seclusion. Kaka added that in the Man-o-nash period Baba seemed to want to open the door and step out of the universe.

Next, Baba showed us the body of the blue bus in which He had travelled all over India, and which had been set on a concrete base for Him to sit in during His seclusion in the Man-o-nash period. Baba had also sat in seclusion in this bus during His forty days' fast in 1949.

Baba then introduced us to Gustadji, who had been

*October 1951-February 1952

with Baba ever since Upasni Maharaj told Baba that He was the Avatar, and instructed Gustadji to follow Baba and do as He said. Gustadji has been on silence now for 27 years, in accordance with Baba's instructions.

Baba next showed us the asbestos cabin that had been made out of two cabins that were on the top of the hill at Pimpalgaon, and in which Baba used to retire during the Man-o-nash period in the daytime. He remarked that He now sleeps there sometimes, and showed us His bed, which consisted of a thin mat and a hard pillow, stretched over the stone floor.

Baba then led us to His "Mast-work" room, a stone building about ten feet square.

"I always use this room for a particular kind of work, known to Me only. Ramjoo lives here now."

Then Baba had Eruch tell us of an incident that occurred during the Man-o-nash period, which had something to do with conflicting orders. Baba was in this stone room, in seclusion, and Eruch, who was on guard during the night, was told not to open the door unless Baba clapped. He was sitting outside on the ground with a lantern and a torch. At 2 a.m. a snake tried to slide under the door of the cabin. Eruch held him fast by the tail with his torch. Just then Baba clapped. If Eruch had obeyed His instructions to open the door immediately, the snake could have entered. So Eruch waited and, fortunately, in a few minutes the snake decided to go elsewhere. But when Eruch entered the cabin, Baba wanted to know why he hadn't obeyed His orders to come immediately when He clapped. Eruch explained, and Baba smiled.

"And I always say," Baba remarked in conclusion, "when there are conflicting orders, always obey the first order."

Then Baba had the boys tell a story of Gustadji's experience with conflicting orders. Baba had been with some of the Mandali to the Girnar mountains for mast-work. Baidul, whom Baba calls the mast expert, and who can, according to Baba, "smell" a *mast*, finds them or takes them to Baba, or Baba to them, as Baba may wish. Baidul had located a *mast* at Girnar, and Baba had come there late at night with a number of the Mandali. The only light they had were some small lamps. They had been moving about for days, from one place to another, sleeping in railway stations, and this night, Baba had decided that they would sleep near the shrine of a Mohammedan saint. They found a small room for Baba, outside of which there was a concrete bench, on which one or the other of the Mandali sat keeping watch. For the last 25 years, wherever Baba rests at night, a watchman is posted outside. Sometimes one man watches all night, sometimes the boys work in shifts. So, this night they sat in shifts on a concrete bench. Baba's instructions were for them to sit there, to awaken each other in turn, and to allow no noise, not even the least, to disturb Him. Sometimes even mosquitoes and flies in flight disturb Him.

At 3 a.m. it was Gustadji's turn to be on watch. All of them had travelled all day, without rest or relaxation; without even having an opportunity to attend to their elimination. From 3 a.m. to 4 a.m., the boys have discovered, Baba usually rests completely, and if they have to attend to anything like elimination, this is usually the safe time to do it. So Gustadji decided that he would try. He was in this unfamiliar place, in almost complete darkness, so he had to grope his way to what he thought would be a good spot to urinate. He had just opened his robe and raised his foot to step off the other side of the bench, when Baba clapped. He rearranged his robe as quickly as he could and went to Baba, who inquired why he was late, and instructed him to sit down and not to move. Later, Baba asked the time and gave Gustadji permission to go. When Gustadji got outside and started again to relieve his discomfort, the sky was clear and Gustadji was amazed to find that just beyond the place where he had raised his foot, was a big lake into which he would have fallen if Baba had not clapped — and, Gustadji being on silence, could not have called for assistance and would probably have drowned.

Baba then led us through the garden, which was lovely, and gave every evidence of being well cared for, to the house where the ladies' quarters were. Rano and Goher met us in the garden, and explained that the house had originally been a rest-house for engineers who were working on the reservoir. The house provided a complete contrast to the men's quarters. They had been primitive; these, for India, were comfortably furnished. We were shown first to the room occupied by Mehera and Mani, neither of whom were present. Rano explained that Mehera and the other girls were mainly responsible for the well-kept garden. Here we were shown pictures of *Manzil-e-Meem;* a chart of the Hierarchy of the Saints; Babawadi, or the school that Baba had for orphans years ago, where they were educated and fed. Then Baba produced several albums of photographs of Himself, which, since there was not time for us to go through them thoroughly at Pimpalgaon, He entrusted to Lud, for us to view at Meherabad at our leisure. He also entrusted to Lud some small boxes in which locks of Baba's hair were kept. These had been cut when He was thirty years old, and were reddish gold in color. People now make lockets and brooches with Baba's hair.

Baba then led the way to the upper floor, and as we passed through the hall, we noticed a beautiful painting of a winged white horse by Marguerite Poley, of California.

We were first taken to Baba's own room, which opens out on the verandah. It was a large simple room, with a wooden bed, where Baba sometimes sleeps. The other rooms were shown to us in turn.

Baba then led us out of the house and up the hill where the cabins used to be into which He used to retire either for *mast*-work or for seclusion. He explained that the hill was not far from Gorakhnath, where Krishna used to play with

Climbing up Tembe Hill, Pimpalgaon

the Gopis, and it was also near Khandoba's temple.

On the way up the hill Baba followed His recent custom of throwing four stones. He led us first to the flat place, just below the top of the hill, where one of the cabins had been during His seclusion and *mast*-work. This was the one where the Mandali had stayed during the day-time. Then all of us, except Will Backett and Charles Purdom, whom Baba ordered to wait, followed Baba up to the summit where the other cabin had been—the one in which He had retired, and in which He did His *mast*-work.

Then Baba led the way down the hill and into the patio of the house, where we all gathered around Him.

"If you are not in trim, you are likely to feel this in your legs for two days," He said.

"You are all really fortunate to have come with Me on the hill, with My leading the way. That is a very dear piece of land, that hill. When I was there I fasted on only very weak tea. The hill is now barren, but a time will come when

Avatar on Tembe (Seclusion) Hill

there will be much construction there by My disciples."

Baba then told us to sit quietly for five minutes, when we would have fruit juice to drink. Baba then referred again to the pictures of Himself and the locks of hair which He had entrusted to Lud, and told him again to show them to us at Meherabad and return them.

"Some of them," interjected Fred Winterfeldt.

"All of them," rejoined Baba, "and more. They will come back with your love."

While we were having fruit juice, reference was made to the various places where Baba had retired in seclusion at different times—Mount Abu, Rishikesh, Hardwar, Angarishi, Panchgani, Khuldabad and Meherabad, all were mentioned.

Then came the most moving event of the day. One of the girls appeared with a large shawl, which she carefully opened. Out of this, she drew an old patched coat, originally brown but practically covered with patches of blue and black. Baba told us that this was the most sacred of His possessions. He had worn it steadily for eight years from 1921 on. This included His period of seclusion in the "jhopdi" in 1922.

"What it has in it will be revealed after I drop the body. Then thousands and thousands of men and women will come to worship."

Next an ancient pair of sandals were produced and, following this, a white robe.

"These are the sandals and the robe that I wore when I wore that coat," Baba said. "The sandals were discarded when I first went up the hill at Meherabad."

Eruch then told us that after Baba had stopped wearing this coat, He used to change his clothes frequently and then would give them away, but these things Baba would not part with. We were also told that these things were produced today for the first time in many years. Even the Mandali had not seen them for a long time.

Baba then asked us how we felt, and said that He would see us between 9 and 9:30 a.m. tomorrow at Meherabad.

"So what would be best," He said just before we left, "would be for you from now on to play with Baba's Love. You have only fifteen days more now to absorb Baba. After you leave, you will be free. You can play, work, be with your family and children as much as you want; but here, now, try to absorb as much of Baba as you can. What I would like, in short, is for you to take Me with you when you go back."

Baba then inquired whether we were getting hungry, and asked what we had had for dinner yesterday. Then He embraced us, and sent us back to Meherabad hill.

Friday, September 17

Baba arrived at twenty minutes after nine, and apologized for being delayed by some printers in Ahmednagar who wanted Him to see their press.

"On very special occasions I hold prayer meetings with a few of My most intimate disciples. Today I shall hold one of these meetings so that you all may be included. So you all will come down the hill with Me, and after prayers we shall come back here. You will see a Zoroastrian, Moslem, Hindu and a special Christian prayer being recited. Then we will close with a prayer of confession and I will come back with you.

"I want to tell you in a few words about Max.* In the interview he told Me something very private and personal, which we both promised each other not to disclose. I also included a description of his state of mind since he met Me two years ago. He then told Me that he really did not want to come, but that something made him come.

" 'And now, Baba,' he said, 'I leave it to you whether to

*Haefliger.

go immediately or to stay until the meeting.'

"I told him to go. He felt very sad, and cried. But I told him to go immediately. He will accordingly leave Bombay on the 22nd of September. He is a very fine man, and I love him very much. Today he sent Me a telegram saying, 'Dear Baba, I humbly apologize for having disappointed you and ask your forgiveness.' I cabled in reply, 'Don't worry. My love and blessings.' This I tell you because dear Purdom wanted to know why Max left.

"On the 20th we go to Sakori, leaving at 7 a.m.; so on that day I want you to rise at 5, breakfast at 6, be ready to leave at 7. We return at 1 p.m. and lunch here.

"Today Sarosh might take you to some place in the evening, but no more excursions from tomorrow on, as I have work for you to do. Did you all see Happy Valley yesterday?"

Fred Frey reports for the group on the excursion to Happy Valley. Baba then turns to Lud Dimpfl and asks, "How do you feel?" After Lud's report Baba directs him to tell Don, and continues, "Why didn't you go to Happy Valley yesterday?" Lud replies that when he was away from the hill the previous day he found himself wishing all the time that he had stayed. Baba continues, "From tomorrow you all stay here and do as I will instruct you today after the prayers. There is not much time left and there is one special thing that I want you all to do."

"Now we will go down the hill," Baba said, and we all followed Him at a brisk pace. We arrived at the ashram at the foot of the hill at 9:45 a.m. At first Baba sat in His big chair at the east end of the large hall, while we sat around Him on the floor. Before beginning the prayers, He had all the doors and windows closed. Then He called Kaikobad Dastur and together they went to the opposite end of the room in front of the large painting of Baba. Both Baba and Dastur washed their hands and face in a bowl of water that was brought to them. Then the prayer began, with Dastur chanting the words and Baba swaying in accompaniment.

At one point Dastur removed the string that was tied around his waist. Then both raised their hands, after which Dastur replaced the string. After this Baba washed His hands again. He placed His hands over Dastur's hands. Dastur then touched Baba's forehead and his own forehead, and again Baba's forehead. At the end Baba touched the ground with His hands.

Zoroastrian Prayer

Translated from the Gujarati

"I begin my prayer by invoking the Name of Yazd: O Lord of Creation, Ahurmazd! Thou art the Source of All Light. Thou Who art All Effulgence and All-Knowing, art the Lord of Lords, the King of Kings, the Creator of all creation, the Preserver and Sustainer!

"O Omnipotent, O the Ancient One and Eternal! Thou art the Giver of all boons and Thou art All-Mercy and All-Wisdom and the Source of All Purity!"

"O the Lord of Creation, Ahurmazd! I invoke Thy Name and ask for Thy Blessings. Let Thy Will be done and Thy Justice be administered, O God Ahurmazd!"

Next came the Moslem prayer. Baba called for a cloth to be spread on the ground in front of His painting and a red scarf with which He covered His head. He and Aloba then stood on the cloth facing in the direction of Mecca. Aloba then began to chant the prayer, which consisted of the prelude to the Quoran and the first verse of the Quoran. The free translation that Aloba and Padri gave us follows:

Moslem Prayer

Prelude — "God is Great! God is Great! God is Great! I bear witness that there is no one greater than God. This is the *word of the Prophet. This is the word of the Prophet. I bear witness and say that Mohammed is the Chosen of God. I bear witness and say that Mohammed is the Chosen of God. Come for prayer. Come for prayer. Come towards success. God is the greatest of all! God is the greatest of all! God is the greatest of all! There is none who is fit to be worshipped but God. There is none who is fit to be worshipped but God. There is none who is fit to be worshipped but God."*

Prayer — *"I begin in the name of God, Who is kind and merciful. All praise be to God, Who is the Preserver of the whole world; Who is kind and merciful. He is the Master of the Day of Resurrection. O God! We pray to You and we seek only Your help. Show us the path of righteousness. Show me the path which will bestow on me Thy mercy, and not calamity, by which I may reach my goal, and not fall in a pit.*

"O Prophet Mohammed! Tell the infidels that I do not pray to whom they pray, and they do not pray to the One to Whom I pray. I neither pray to the One to whom you pray, nor do you pray to the One to whom I pray. Your religion is with you, mine is with me. Holy is my God, Who is also Mighty. God has heard the one who has praised Him. O my God! All praise should be attributed to You. My God is high and holy. All thoughts, words and deeds are for God. My obeisance to you, Prophet Mohammed, on whom is bestowed the grace of God. May that grace descend also on me, and on His believers. I bear witness that there is none greater than God, and that Mohammed is the Prophet of God."

All during this prayer, Baba's fingers were moving and at times, He gesticulated with His right hand. Several times Aloba raised his arms, bowed, kneeled and prostrated himself.

Next in succession came the Hindu prayer, which was chanted by Nilu and Vishnu, who stood alongside of Baba, facing His portrait. The prayer was in Sanskrit. During this prayer Baba also swayed, moved the fingers of His right hand and swung His right hand at intervals. At one time, He salaamed, and frequently He raised His hands to His head. At the end of the prayer He touched the ground with His hands. The translation of the prayer follows.

A Hymn in Praise of the Ten Incarnations
Translated from the Sanskrit

1. I bow to Thee, O Lord, Who art the Ruler, the Primaeval Being, the (absolute) Male (i.e. Spirit), the Cause of the creation, and preservation and destruction of the universe, and Who art the Animating Principle, taking bodily form to satisfy the desire of Thy devotees, and Who (in Thy Form of Vishnu the Preserver) sleepest on (Sesha), the King of Cobras, and Whose vehicle is Garud, the King of Birds.

2. I worship Thee, oh Supreme Brahman, in Thy form of the great Fish who moved here and there with ease in the oceans at the time of the end of the Age (cycle), Who directed all to follow the righteous path, Who killed that demon and took away the Vedas from him (i.e. rescued), and Who protected the downtrodden.

3. I worship the extremely pure form of the huge Tortoise which thought its.limbs were mildly scratched (to remove an itching sensation) when it bore the (spinning) Mandar Mountain (used as a churning rod) on its extensive back when the milky ocean was being churned (for nectar) by gods.

4. I bow to the Lord Who is fit to be worshipped in His form of the huge primaeval Boar which came out from the nostrils of the Creator (i.e. the God Brahma), and which lighted up the earth (sinking in the oceans) from the infernal regions, and which ended the life-span of the demon Hiranyaksha in a duel.

5. I praise God in the form of the Man-lion who was terrible (to

behold), who manifested his form from out of a pillar in the royal court, who was praised by gods like Brahma, who were bent low before him, who is the lord (husband) of the Goddess Laksmi (of wealth and prosperity), and who brought about the destruction of demons.

6. *I bow to the Lord in His form of Vaman (the Dwarf), who had a beautiful appearance, who conquered the three worlds from Bali, the king of demons, outwitting him by begging from him just as small a bit of ground as could be covered by three footsteps, and who purified the whole universe by the streams of water (of the river Ganges) which flowed forth from His lotus-like foot (at the moment of stepping in the sky).*

7. *I praise Parashurama, who was eminent even among mighty heroes, who slew King Kartaveerya, who had no other companion except his war-axe (on the battlefield), who was destroyer of the (haughty) war-like race of the Kshatriyas, and who gives the four-fold end of life (viz.: religious merit, wealth, fulfillment of desires, and the final emancipation).*

8. *I worship Ramachandra, who gives prosperity to his devotees, who is fit to be worshipped, who has a smiling face, who is the slayer of the supremely egoistic demons, including the ten-headed Ravana; who is the demolisher of this worldly existence (the mundane life), and who is an ornament to the Solar Dynasty.*

9. *I worship God Krishna, the son of Vasudeo, who was the delight of (his mother) Devaki, who had come down to this earth when he was beseeched by the God Brahma, for the destruction of the armies of the circle of kings who had become a burden to the earth; who was a joy to the city of cow-herds, and who played (when a child) in the house of Nanda.*

10. *I worship the Lord in His Incarnation of Buddha, whose life was mysterious, who proclaimed a religion whose most*

important element is non-injury, who was proficient in censuring the Vedic scriptures which ordained sacrifices (in which beasts were killed as oblations to gods), who was the son of Jina, and who manifested himself in the dynasty of Keekata.

11. I bow down to the incarnation Kalki, who is yet to come in this terribly sinful Kali-Age, who is devoid of all religious rituals like the sacrifices, who will be riding a horse, who will have a destructive sword in his hand, and who will cause the destruction of the multitude of wicked non-believers.

12. I always in my heart contemplate on Thee, O Supreme Brahman, Thou who art birthless, deathless, of the triple form of Existence, Spirit and Joy, Who are beyond thought and speech, Who art approachable by the meditation of Sages, Who pervadest the whole universe, Who art without blemish and without attributes.

Baba then called Eruch and Don. All three faced the portrait and Eruch read the special Christian prayer, at the end of which Baba touched the ground. The prayer follows:

Christian Prayer

In the name of the Father, and of the Son, and of the Holy Ghost:
O Lord! Hear my prayer and let my cry come unto Thee:
Thou who art the God of the God, the Father Almighty, art the
    Father Everlasting!
O God! Almighty Father! The Lord of Lords! The King of
    Kings! All the earth doth worship Thee.
To Thee All Angels, To Thee the Heavens and All Powers,
To Thee All Saints and All Beings with unceasing voice do cry:
    The Holy! The Holy of Holies!
Full are the Heavens and the Earth, of the Majesty of Thy Glory.
Thou the Glorious! Thou the Exalted Effulgence;

Thou the Praiseworthy in the Assemblage of the Prophets;
Thou the Celestial Beauty! art the Eternal Song of Thy Lovers.
Thou Who art acknowledged, praised and worshipped throughout
the World, in all Churches, Synagogues, Mosques, Temples
and Pagodas: To Thee I most humbly bow down.
Thou of Unbounded Majesty! art the Father of the Creation;
Thy True Adorable and Only Begotten Son, The Christ, art the
King of Glory, the Saviour of Mankind, The Ancient One,
The Highest of the High!
O Christ! The Messiah! Thou of the Father Everlasting art the
Son Everlasting:
Thou O Most Merciful Lord! has taken upon Thee to deliver
Man from bondage, to Eternal Glory:
O The Ancient One! The Redeemer! Thou, having first overcome
the Sting of Ignorance, didst open to all the kingdom of
Bliss, Knowledge and Power;
I most humbly praise Thee, O My God!
I Most Firmly Acknowledge Thee, O My God!
O My Soul of Soul! I believe in Thee, because Thou art Truth
Itself;
I worship Thee, O Highest of the High; Because Thou art the
Only One worthy of Adoration: I love Thee above all things
and beings, because Thou art Love Divine Itself;
I beseech Thee, because Thou art Mercy Itself;
I offer Thee all my thoughts, words and actions, my sufferings and
my joys, because Thou art the Only Beloved:
I therefore beseech Thee, my God! My Lord of Lords! The Highest
of the High! The Ancient One! to have mercy on me,
according to Thy Unbounded Mercy, and let my cry come
unto Thee:
O My Beloved! Suffer me not to be separated from Thee for ever
and ever!

Amen!

Baba sends Don out to wash his hands, pacing up and down until he returns. Then he and Baba both face the portrait and Don reads the Prayer of Repentance, at the conclusion of which Baba touches both His forehead and the ground, and bows down before His picture.

Prelude

"O the Eternally Benevolent Paramatma! O All-Merciful Allah! O The Most Merciful God Almighty! O Giver of all boons, Yazdan! Being fully aware of Your absolute Independence and Your absolute Indifference, Baba, with all humbleness, implores You, O All-Merciful God! to accept the Prayer of Repentance from Him on behalf of all His lovers and on behalf of all who are worthy of being forgiven.

The Prayer of Repentance

We repent, O God Most Merciful; for all our sins; for every thought that was false or unjust or unclean; for every word spoken that ought not to have been spoken; for every deed done that ought not to have been done.

We repent for every deed and word and thought inspired by selfishness, and for every deed and word and thought inspired by hatred.

We repent most specially for every lustful thought and every lustful action; for every lie; for all hypocrisy; for every promise given but not fulfilled, and for all slander and backbiting.

Most specially also, we repent for every action that has brought ruin to others; for every word and deed that has given others pain; and for every wish that pain should befall others.

In your Unbounded Mercy! We ask you to forgive us, O God! for all these sins committed by us, and to forgive us for our constant failures to think and speak and act according to Your Will.

At the conclusion of the prayer of confession, Baba ordered the doors and windows to be opened and resumed His seat in His big chair, while we sat around on the floor. "Today," He spelt out on His alphabet board, "Today, you have joined God praying to God. I and God are one. Now we go up the hill."

On the way up the hill, Baba stopped to show us Don's dispensary. "This is Don's dispensary," He said. "And I have nothing to worry about regarding health, because here is the doctor and he is most dear to Me. The faith and love with which this dear son of Mine has stuck to Me is unique. As I told you yesterday, if anything bothers you, if even the slightest thing is wrong with you, tell Don."

We returned to the lounge at the top of the hill at 11 a.m. Rano Gayley, who had come from Pimpalgaon with Baba, showed us two symbolic paintings which she had executed under Baba's direction, and three photographs of Baba, as a boy, as a young man in college, and in the "Prem Ashram" days.

"From tomorrow on," Baba began, after the pictures had been shown, "I want you all to think exclusively of Me for a half hour every day for seven days. You should each sit aloof from the others, and select your own spot, close your eyes and just try to bring Baba's figure before your mind's eye. If you find that you cannot do that, then just look at My picture and mentally repeat 'Baba.' If thoughts bother you, don't be concerned; let them come and go, but try your best to keep Baba's figure clearly in your mind's eye. Select spots where you will not be disturbed. One-half hour, silent contemplation, for seven days beginning from tomorrow. Is there anyone who wants to ask about this?"

Lud asked what to do about mosquitoes! Baba said we could get under our mosquito nets.

"You must be undisturbed. For seven days, for a half

hour a day, in Baba's atmosphere, I want you to do this whole-heartedly. From 9 to 9:30 a.m. daily, on the 18th, 19th, 21st, 22nd, 23rd, 24th, and 25th. From the 26th I will not be available, as I will have many things to attend to for the meetings."

Baba then called Savak and told him to see that we were undisturbed during this half-hour meditation. Turning to us, He concluded His remarks on this subject by saying, "Do it so whole-heartedly that I must feel it here," and He pointed to His heart.

"I will only give points today — no explanation. Tomorrow, if time permits, I will explain about God and the Universe, Reality and Illusion, the One and the Many, Substance and Shadow, Everything and Nothing, Knowledge and Ignorance, and the gap between the seven descents and the seven ascents.

"Christ and His inner circle, and the Christian mystics, all stressed purity of heart. Mohammed and His *Imams* also stressed purity of heart. So did Zoroaster and the Magis; so did Krishna and His companions, and the Vedantists. So does Baba stress purity of heart. Today we shall see what this means — what the heart is — what the mind is. Is it only the organ that is meant, or something deeper? A Sufi said: "The Abode of Love is infinitely higher than the domain of intellect. He alone, out of the millions and billions of people, can touch and kiss the threshold of the Beloved who carries his life in his sleeves.' This is the literal translation. What it means is that if you want to see your beloved God, you must go before Him with your head in the palm of your hand. It means that the intellect can never attain to the One Who transcends the mind. So we now understand that God can not be understood. He is not visible, because He is infinitely visible to that eye which has no veil of desires, or of ego, over it. The mind has a dual function, which I have explained at length in *God Speaks*. The first function is that of thinking. The impressions that lie dormant have to be worked out, and so they appear as thoughts. This thinking function of mind is known to the Vedantists as 'Manas.'

"The second function of mind includes all feelings and emotions. This is called 'Antahkarana.' That means the heart. So what is known as the heart is actually the second functioning of the mind itself.

"The impressions, called 'Sanskaras,' are spent both through thinking and through feeling. In the first functioning of the mind are included thoughts of all kinds. In the second functioning of the mind, that is heart, are included all feelings and desires — feelings of joy, pain disappointment, happiness, shock, all belong to this 'Antahkarana.'

"In sound sleep, the impressions that have been registered in the mind lie in a latent, dormant state. We won't discuss dreams now; they have all been explained in *God Speaks*. What wakes you up from sound sleep? The impressions of actions done, and these impressions are spent first by thoughts, then by desires, then by actions. So Krishna, in His Gita, said, 'Let impressions be spent only through thoughts.' Then no new impressions will be formed. If you can not do this, then let the impressions be spent through desires, longings, feelings, but not through actions. Then new impressions will be formed, but they will not be so deep. If impressions lead to action, then new and stronger impressions are bound to be formed. This means that the first functioning of the mind is not important in so far as spending impressions is concerned. It is natural. But the second functioning of the mind, which is generally called the heart, is important because it is the seat of desires, and unless the heart is void of all desires and all feelings, unless the heart is pure and naked, God, Who is your innermost Self, can not reveal Himself. Is this clear?"

Malcolm asked, "What about repressions?" Baba replied, "Do not ask this now."

"God is your innermost Self. That means that behind this limited body, you have within you energy and mind, with both its functions. You as you — the ego — are also there. Behind all this, imagine God as infinite in space. Try to grasp what this means. You have this idea of yourself as body; you feel happy, depressed, hungry. You, you, you. This you think to be yourself; but behind this you, there is something that can not be got rid of, even if the body is not there. If both your hands or both your legs were to be cut off, you would still exist as you. That means that you are not this body. In sound sleep, you are unconscious of your body, but you still exist; so you are not this body. Who then is this you? This you is your innermost Self. We must find, in our own self, this important 'I.'

"Who am I? I have said that I am not this body. Then who am I? I might be energy; but when I do not move, do not act — when I am unconscious — energy does not manifest itself; yet I still exist. So I am not energy.

"I might be mind. But the same applies here. When I am unconscious, in sound sleep, and the mind is still, the mind is not functioning, but I still exist; so I am also not mind. Then who am I? Try to grasp this. Let us try to understand what can not be understood. I am that which is not body, not energy, not mind.

"In sound sleep, what do you experience? Nothing. That is you. I will now tell you something that is not said, that is not written, that must not be said, but I say it. *I am sound sleep.* Why? If I am not body, energy, mind, then I am that which has no body, energy, mind; and only sound sleep means that. Only sound sleep answers the question. In sound sleep you are not body, not energy, not mind, and yet the body is there, energy is there, mind is there. Only the consciousness of body, of energy, of mind is not there.

"I will now go to the first point and return to this later. The original state of the beginningless Beginning was the infinite sound-sleep state of the Infinite One. In the beginningless Beginning, when there was no creation, no universe — not even nothing — there was only the state of 'was.'

"Then started the Ten States of God, which you will find described in *God Speaks*. During the processes of evolution and reincarnation, impressions were gathered; body, energy and mind developed, and the soul, in spite of its infinite state, experienced itself as the finite body, as energy, and as mind, due to these impressions.

"Now we return. In sound sleep, Malcolm is not conscious of body, energy, mind, and only Malcolm as real Malcolm exists. The important point is that Malcolm in the sound-sleep state exists as 'I am Malcolm,' and is absolutely unconscious of this 'I-ness.' The ego in the sound-sleep or absolute-unconscious state is called 'The Natural Ego.' There are three kinds of ego; the first is the Natural Ego.

"What wakes you up from sound sleep? The impressions that lie on your mind. They say, 'Malcolm, wake up! We want to be spent.' So Malcolm wakes up and spends the impressions through thinking, desiring, acting; and Malcolm, while spending the impressions, thinks 'I am this body.' This 'I' is called the 'False Ego.' Let us not go too deeply into this. Malcolm, who really is Malcolm, and not this body, according to impressions, takes one form after another, and goes on spending new impressions. But that is a different chapter.

"While spending old impressions, new impressions are formed, which also need spending; so, ever new forms are taken, according to good and bad impressions — man, woman, beautiful, ugly, rich, poor, strong, weak, and so forth. They are like different clothes, which you alternately wear and discard, and all along, this False Ego persists.

"Then comes a time when the impressions grow fainter and fainter, scarcer and scarcer. Eventually they become so faint that they fade away completely, and when impressions are not there, mind's functioning is stopped. The heart is now naked and pure, because there are no desires, no longings, no feelings; yet *you* are still there. Then the 'I,' void of all impressions, has no bindings, no limits. It now experiences that state which is above mind, because the mind is no longer there. It experiences the Infinite Original State of Real 'I'-ness. This ego is called the Real Ego, and just as with the False Ego, Malcolm said, 'I am this body — or I am this energy — or I am this mind' — now Malcolm says 'I am God.'

"So there is the Natural Ego, the False Ego and the Real Ego. Only the pure in heart can see God.

"What I wanted to explain is new — not these things. This was what Purdom asked about — what being pure in heart meant.

"All this which I have explained will take you nowhere, because how can one explain One Whom the mind cannot grasp?

"There is a bird of paradise which is said never to come to earth. Hafiz said 'God is like the bird of paradise. Don't try to snare Him by spreading the net of intellect. In that net you will find nothing but wind.' And so it is said, 'Only love, and God will be yours.' Not intellect, but love. So however much I may explain, God can not be explained; but, if I should wish it, in a split second you would see God and you would know.

"Ramakrishna did not speak any language except Bengali. He could not read; He was what they call illiterate. Yet, in an instant, He gained All Knowledge. Flocks of very literate and learned people gathered around Him without understanding a thing He said. So love. The secret is, in a few words — when you are there, God is not. Now to explain and to understand, you must be there, and when you are there, God is not. So explanations and understandings mean you drive away God, instead of drawing Him in. When you understand you have not understood God. God is.

" 'My one and the same Beloved,' it is said, 'appears in different guises and garbs, and with different names, and appears to be always different, and yet He is one and the same Beloved.'

"You have to become what you already are. You are God, but you must become God. Christ humiliated Himself, God Himself crucified Himself, to teach this: through love, become what you already are.

"Emperor Janak, Sita's father, was also known to be a Perfect Master. During his reign, there was a youth from outside his empire who longed desperately to see God. 'I must see Him,' he said, 'as clearly as I see these external things.' And he decided to see Janak and to ask his help. For two months he walked through sun and rain without food. This was seven thousand years ago. There were no automobiles and airplanes then. Finally he arrived at the courtyard of Janak's palace. The guards accosted him and stopped him. He stood outside the wall, crying aloud for Janak, shouting his name, his glory and his fame. At last Janak heard him, and asked his ministers to inquire who he was.

" 'I am a lover of God,' he replied, 'I want to see God. Janak must show me God.'

"Janak had him brought in and said to his ministers, 'Throw him in prison.' So he was thrown in jail. The youth thought, 'This Janak, who calls himself all-knowing, must know that I am seeking God, yet he sends me to prison.' After a few days during which the youth had had no food or drink, Janak ordered him brought to audience. Janak saluted him with folded hands, and ordered his ministers to give him a bath, to feed him, and to treat him like a prince. He was brought back to the palace and seated on Janak's throne. 'Let him enjoy this state for three days,' said Janak,

"The youth did not grasp what Janak had in mind. He did not know how to manage the affairs of state. Poor people came begging, ministers came for advice; he didn't know what to do, so he just kept quiet. Finally he appealed to the ministers to ask Janak to free him from this uncomfortable position. Janak came, ordered him to get down from the throne, and asked which he preferred, life in prison or life on the throne. The boy said, 'They are both prisons, but of different kinds.' Janak then directed him to go, and to return after twelve years.

"The youth left the palace, roamed about India, became a rich man, and took the name of Kalyan, which means 'happy in every respect.' After twelve years he returned to Janak, this time rich and prosperous. The guards again checked him, asking who he was. 'I am the rich Kalyan' he said. Janak, on hearing this, sent word for him to go away for a few more years. So Kalyan returned home and, in the course of time, he lost everything that he possessed. After twelve years he returned to Janak who again asked who he was. 'I am the miserable Kalyan,' he replied. Janak then sent him away again for twelve more months.

"During this time Kalyan started pondering: 'What is this? When I first went to Janak, I had nothing but I wanted to see God. Then I was thrown into prison. Then I was placed on the throne. Then I became rich. Then I became poor. What does all this mean?'

"When he returned to Janak's palace after twelve months, one of the guards took pity on him and said, 'You fool! This time when Janak asks who you are, say "I don't know."' Kalyan followed this advice. Janak then turned his gaze upon him and he lost consciousness of all bodies, of the whole world, and yet remained conscious of his own Self as the Infinite God.

"The meaning of this is, — unless you lose the 'I,' you can not see and become God, because where you are, God is not.

"Now about Myself. When I was a boy I did not know anything. I had nothing to do with spirituality. My father, who was a dervish, had roamed throughout India and Persia, begging and contemplating God. He taught Me some verses from Hafiz and other poets, but I had no interest in all this. I preferred marbles, kites, cricket. But in all the games that I played, I found Myself naturally the leader of others.

"Yet one day, when a friend gave Me a small booklet on the Buddha, I opened the book to the place that told about the second coming of the Buddha as Maitreya, the Lord of Mercy, and I realized all of a sudden, 'I am that, actually,' and I felt it deep within Me. Then I forgot about it, and years passed by.

"Babajan called Me one day as I was cycling past Her tree, and She kissed Me on the forehead; and for nine months, God knows, I was in that state to which very, very few go, even in cycles of time. I had no consciousness of My body, or of anything else. I roamed about, taking no food. My mother thought I was mad, and called the doctor. My father understood, but said nothing. The doctors could not do anything. I did not sleep, because I was unconscious; and then what happened is very rare. It is only for Avatars, who take on themselves the suffering of the world. I took no food but tea, which My elder brother Jamshed, who loved Me very much, gave Me. One day, all of a sudden, I felt nature's call. I wanted to move my bowels, but it was impossible because I had not had any food. I sat there and had no stool. Then I saw, with these gross eyes of Mine, circles and circles, whole universes. From that moment, instead of the Divine Bliss that I was in for the nine months, I was in such tortures that no one in the world can understand. I used to bang My head to relieve My pain. I scarred My head on floors and walls. I could not contain Myself. It was as if the whole universe was on My head. I used to break windows open with My forehead.

"Then I was drawn out to Sai Baba. It was an intense urge. Sai Baba directed Me to Upasni Maharaj. He picked up a stone and hit Me on the head. All at once, I felt calm; and I knew I was the Ancient One. Then seven years passed, and one day Maharaj folded His hands and said, 'Merwan, you are the Avatar.'

"I am now infinitely enjoying bliss and infinitely

suffering at the same time. As soon as I drop My body, I will go to My abode of Infinite Bliss. I suffer and suffer. From October, for three months, will be the climax of My sufferings, and then the world will recognize Me.

"Sometimes I feel, 'Why explain anything?' Just come, sit down, you all be here, be quiet, and be in company with Baba. Sometimes I feel like explaining things. I wonder which is better. What shall we do? Shall we go on explaining, or shall we be quiet?"

We also were divided on this subject, so Baba decided that one day He would explain, and on the next day we would be quiet with Him.

"Your work has to be defined," He continued. "It has to be practical and yet divine; practical in the sense that in every life it can be achieved, not just sitting quiet, aloof, renouncing the world. I will give you new and original aspects of the same truth.

"A form of Zoroastrian prayer is called *Kusti*. All four prayers say the same thing. Since Babajan kissed Me on the forehead, I bow down to My own Self. Why?"

Someone said, "Because there is nothing else to bow down to."

"That is My actual, continual experience," Baba resumed. "What is needed is to become, not only to see. You have to become what you already are. You are God, but you have to know how to become God; and Christ humiliated Himself, God Himself crucified Himself, to teach this: — through love, become what you already are."

Saturday, September 18

From 9 to 9:30 a.m., we all sat quietly, thinking of Baba and trying to visualize His figure in our mind's eye.

At 10:05 a.m. Baba started walking up the hill. On the way up the road, He stooped down three times, picked up a stone each time, and threw it into the grass. At the top of the hill He greeted each of us warmly, clasping our hands.

Then He led us directly to the lounge. Meherji followed with an oriental rug, which he spread on the divan for Baba to sit on, a phonograph and some records. Eruch followed with letters for the group.

Baba began by inquiring whether we all sat in contemplation of Him from 9 to 9:30 a.m. After each had answered in turn and described his experience with this assignment, Baba began to speak.

"Today I will explain about trance and inner sight — *Samadhi*. Trance, which the Sufis term '*Haal*' and Vedantists term '*Bhav*,' is just a momentary ecstasy which, in the true spiritual sense, has no great value. During this state of *Haal* one feels unconscious of his surroundings and of his own body, but is conscious of an overpowering force of bliss pouring in on his soul. As soon as this *Bhav* ends, he is just his ordinary self. There are four different types of *Samadhi*, — *Yoga Samadhi*, *Tantrika Samadhi*, *Nirvikalpa Samadhi* and *Sahaj Samadhi*.

"*Yoga Samadhi* and *Tantrika Samadhi* have no importance, spiritually. In these *Samadhis*, one feels at peace with everything and everyone, and finally finds his mind still; but as soon as this *Samadhi* is over, he is again his ordinary self. Most *Yogis*, after these *Samadhis*, feel the strain of illusion even more. It is like taking intoxicants; one feels in harmony with everything for a while, but when the intoxication is over, one gets a headache. So, *Yoga Samadhi*, *Tantrika Samadhi* are like getting drunk completely. One feels like an emperor, as if one could do anything; but as soon as it is over, one feels the stress and strain again.

"In *Nirvikalpa Samadhi*, which the Sufis call '*Fana*,' and which means passing away from selfhood to the union with God, the soul identifies itself with God. This *Samadhi* is the real *Samadhi*, *Fana*. Here one becomes God. God's Knowledge is his knowledge, God's Bliss is his bliss, God's Power is his power, God's Beauty is his beauty. During this *Samadhi*, he has no consciousness of body, energy, mind, universe, but is only conscious of the Self as God. Very,

very few, it is said, get this *Nirvikalpa Samadhi*, and these few only rarely.

"It is said: 'After cycles and cycles, one gets 'Fana.' This one is then called 'Fana-fillah,' or one who has been made one with God. Very few such regain normal consciousness; but one who does regain normal consciousness has *Sahaj Samadhi*. To have *Sahaj Samadhi* means that spontaneously and simultaneously one is always in *Nirvikalpa Samadhi*, and yet is also fully conscious of the universe. Such a one, when he speaks, eats, moves about, plays, or does anything, is enjoying *Nirvikalpa Samadhi* all the time. He is called a 'Qutub' which, in Persian, means the Center of everything — the pivot. He is now on every plane of consciousness, one with God, even on the level of an ant, and simultaneously he is functioning in the gross, subtle and mental worlds; yet he is above everything. *Sahaj Samadhi* means effortless Oneness. It is as simple and automatic as moving the hands or winking the eyelids.

"Tomorrow, if you remind Me — I don't promise — I will tell you how, when thinking of Me, you can still do everything you need to do in the world. This is not *Sahaj Samadhi*, but *Sahaj Dhyan*. Even while eating, drinking, working, while looking at motion pictures, or attending to your business, you will still feel that Baba is with you. This is *Sahaj Dhyan*.

"Tomorrow, when we play the Indian records, I intend to explain many things, if I am in a good mood. Today, let us keep silence, but at the same time listen to some English recordings. I am very fond of music, but have not had time to listen recently. The girls made Me bring these records. While the records are being played, be here in this room mentally, and not elsewhere. Kabir said, 'Any music is the seventh shadow of that Word.' In *God Speaks* I deal with this. As soon as I break My silence, that first Word will make your hearts vibrate."

The following records were then played:

Marian Anderson — "I know the Lord has His hands

on me, and I am fancying that Heaven is my home." Fritz Kreisler — A selection from "The Student Prince," and "Indian Love Call." Richard Crookes — "The Song of Songs," and "Love and Love Alone." Yma Sumac — "Lure of the Unknown Love," and "Virgin of the Sun God."

Some of the group didn't care especially about Yma Sumac, but Baba said, "As long as it goes to the highest and goes to the lowest, I like it. It reminds Me of My original state. I feel happy."

Now followed a song by Yma Sumac which Dana Field translated as "I love only Thee, I worship only Thee, to Thee only I surrender the key to my treasure;" and Baba continued, "He who could do this would know Me."

"This reminds Me, when I drop this body, which will come about through violence, not one will be near Me at that time — none of My lovers, none of My Mandali — only those who would kill this body. The circumstances will be so created that in the confusion Baba will not find one near Him. Only afterward they will flock around. It is staring Me in the face. It might happen before the end of the year — My breaking the silence, dropping the body, and all this. In the meeting, I will speak at length about this."

Here followed another record of Yma Sumac: "High Andes," and "Monkeys." At the end of this record, Baba turned to Purdom and said, "Dear Charles, can anyone imagine how I am here and simultaneously everywhere? And I am being crucified every moment, and I would willingly die a million deaths to make someone love our Beloved God, Who alone is worthy of our love." Purdom replies that he can imagine, but that is all.

Baba asks for another Yma Sumac record, and "The Dance of the Winds" and "The Chant of the Chosen Maidens" are played. In the midst of one of these, a card is sent to Baba which reads, in part, "If I could see you only for a moment, I would be eternally grateful." The signature is that of a young Japanese, K. Hitaker, from Tokyo.

Baba had Eruch usher him in. Deeply moved, he prostrated himself before Baba, and Baba bade him rise.

"I don't allow anyone to come up on the hill," He commented wryly. Then He called Lud to Him and embraced him. Lud returned to his seat in tears. In fact, we were all probably on the verge of tears. Baba then gave Hitaker His own grapefruit juice to drink, and said, "You have come far, drink it all."

When Hitaker had finished drinking, Baba asked him, "Why did you come such a long distance? Baba is everywhere."

"I would like to have you come to Japan," Hitaker replied.

"After seven hundred years I will come to Japan," said Baba.

Hitaker later told Eruch that he had heard of Baba years ago from a Dr. Muir, who was the leader of a Theosophical group in Japan, and that he had been wanting, longing to meet Baba ever since. He was invited to India by the Japanese Ambassador, to whom he is related, and he seized this opportunity to make contact with Baba. He had now to return to Calcutta to get an extension of his visa, so Baba told him to go to Calcutta today, arriving there on the 22nd, and leaving on the 24th to be back in Meherabad on the 28th in time for the meetings.

Bill LePage and John Ballantyne were then ordered by Baba to sit in His tomb from midnight to 12:30, mentally repeating Baba's name, with eyes open and mouth shut. Baba told Francis that he would be responsible for them if they should fall in the crypt, and asked Francis what he would do if that happened. Francis replied, "It isn't what I would do, but what You would do to me, that matters."

Baba said later that after the meetings of the 29th and 30th, He might have Hitaker sit alone in one place for seven days without food or drink. "And," said Baba, "if he does this, I may give him just a tiny glimpse of Me. He is a fine boy, and he is very much in love with Truth. I have drawn him. He has no idea how."

Baba then sent us to lunch at ten minutes to one, and stayed with us while we were eating, passing behind us and patting us each once on the shoulder. He called Hitaker to Him several times for short conversations.

Sunday, September 19

Baba arrives at 10:25 a.m. on foot from Meherabad. It is a soft, cloudy morning. He smiles, but is suffering. He says that today Hé will sit for many hours. "Today I have plenty of time, let us go slow. From tomorrow I have no time."

He says, "Health: give Me your reports." He asks each one individually; some have little complaints and He tells them to see Don. "I want you all to be well and strong for the 29th and 30th. I feel funny today," He said. "I sometimes can not describe My feelings; certain things even I can not describe. For example, when I was walking up here I threw stones. Years ago, I used to throw stones. At every step I would stoop down, pick up a stone, and throw it. I do it now sometimes. Why I do so I can not say. What do you think? — Divine Play," is Baba's answer.

He asks, "What do you feel when I come?" A young Australian, Bill LePage, says, "A funny feeling." Baba can not understand what he means. He asks, "Did you keep your eyes open when you sat for half an hour last night?" "Yes." "What did you feel?" "My heart pounded all the time, and I could not say Your Name." "What was there to frighten you?" "I had images of the outside world." The other young Australian said, "I had a feeling that there was no ventilation when the door was closed. I felt nothing."

Baba asked if they would do it every night for seven nights. They said, "Yes." "Do not be frightened," said Baba, "there is nothing to fear. Don't force your attention; keep awake and don't move. Even if a snake comes, let it pass by. And love Baba during these half hours. Fear means no love.

Think of Baba from the bottom of your hearts; after seven nights you will see Baba. Why this fear, Francis? Francis of Assissi and Francis Xavier loved Christ with all their might, and what they suffered none of you can guess; but fear was foreign to them. Do not fear, love me. Don't be bothered; think of Baba; be happy. So from tonight, Francis, see that they sit there and close the door."

Just then a boy comes in with an envelope. Baba takes the envelope and tells him to go. The boy obeys literally.

He went on to say, "Francis, you sell all and follow the Cross. I am in a peculiar mood. We will have a vague talk, moving from one subject to another. I seldom sleep till after 3 o'clock in the morning. When I am in seclusion, the night watchman is called every few minutes until then. When do you all go to sleep? At ten. Don't let the two young men sit tonight, as you have to be up so early, but from tomorrow." Baba gives Ludwig tablets to enable him to sleep: they were what the boy had brought.

"You asked about the planes," He said to Malcolm. "Planes mean what?" Malcolm answers, "States of consciousness." Baba replied, "This present state of yours is gross consciousness; the gross senses are used, and you have the gross experiences of eating, drinking, and moving about. This is the gross world; it is not the gross plane. Although the consciousness is gross, it is not the gross plane. *Manzil* means destination or goal; *Muqam* means place of stay or state. You must differentiate. You are in the gross *manzil* and there are innumerable *muqam* states. Meherabad is a *muqam* where you experience with the gross senses. When you are in America, France, England, the *manzil* is the same — gross — but the *muqam* is different, and you have different experiences of the gross world in each place. If a man in Arangaon, who seldom even visits Ahmednagar, were blindfolded, put in a plane, and set down on Broadway in the night, his experiences would be fantastic to him because of the different *muqam*, but it would be the same *manzil*.

"Now, even in the gross *manzil*, glimpses of the subtle plane are possible. There are three *manzils* in the subtle plane. Now what happens? The human being with gross senses experiences the first *manzil* of the subtle plane in a hazy way, because of the gross senses; because experience of the subtle plane can not be fully gained except through the subtle senses. The gross experiences are hazy: one sees colors, and they disappear; circles of different kinds; wonderful perfumes never smelled before; one hears celestial music; one is inspired; but it all disappears. You must understand that all *manzils*, all *muqams*, and all these experiences are illusions. Only God is real. That is the fundamental fact.

"When the soul, through its Herculean efforts or by the grace of a *Guru* (not a Perfect Master), gets into the first plane, it does not mean that it enters another sphere. Its consciousness is raised, and it can use its subtle senses fully. What was smelt, heard, seen temporarily, is now smelt, heard and seen continually. It is now in the first *manzil* of the subtle world. We call it world, because just as the gross world has innumerable *muqams*, so has the subtle world. In the first *manzil* of the subtle world, through subtle senses, the soul sees different sights, has different smells and has different experiences (just as you have different foods in Meherabad, different smells, and different languages from what you were used to), according to the different *muqams*. In the subtle plane, the first *manzil* has innumerable *muqams*. You feel differently here from what you do in your homes with your family and children, though you are still in the gross world. So, in the subtle plane, in the first *manzil*, the soul sees wonderful things, and gets enchanted, it loses its gross consciousness, and it begins to hear subtle music, and to see subtle sights and to enjoy them. But if the soul is wise, through good fortune, or the *Guru* is capable, the soul leaves the first *manzil* and enters the second *manzil* of the subtle plane. In that *manzil* the soul sees, hears and smells through the subtle senses more intensely, and the *muqams* of the subtle sphere appear more agreeable. In the second *manzil* the soul becomes so enchanted and is so overpowered that everything is a billion times brighter than the sun, and a million times colder than the moon.

"The soul gets enveloped in this light, and hears the voices and smells the scents so intensely and so overpoweringly that it enters it completely. This is called the spiritual talisman. One has no consciousness of the gross sphere.

"If the *Murshid* (or *Guru*) is not capable, and if its past impressions do not allow it to proceed, the soul drops the body, takes another form, and comes back in the same state of consciousness. Yet it is pure illusion.

"If the *Guru* is adept, he advances the soul, and the third *manzil* is reached. Consciousness is still subtle. The *muqams* are the same *muqams*. The subtle senses are now in their most intense phase. But the innumerable sights and sounds of the innumerable *muqams* do not overpower the soul. It has now full control over the senses and its experiences, not only in the gross *manzil*, but also in the two previous subtle *manzils*. It is now energy personified. All this is dealt with in *God Speaks*. The soul still has its gross body, and is still in the gross world, but functions simultaneously in the subtle world. It uses its gross and subtle senses simultaneously. If Francis were in the third *manzil* of the subtle plane, and at the same time expressing the *muqams* of the third *manzil*, he would have gross and subtle consciousness simultaneously: he would have infinite energy under his control in the gross world. Yet our poor Francis would still be in illusion.

"The day after tomorrow we will talk about the 4th, 5th and 6th planes. Until we arrive at Reality, and know that all this is *tamasha* — farce. Lovers of God do not care for this *tamasha*. Yogis of the first *manzil* of the subtle plane can stop their pulses or live underground, or raise their gross bodies in the air, or even live for 500 years; but it is all illusion and farce. The seventh *manzil* is called *maksood*, the Goal, where the soul is free from illusion and becomes one with God. I will make it clear, when we come to the seventh *manzil*, that all is within you — all *manzils*, all *muqams* are within you, for God is within you. When you go outside this room you see the surrounding country. Why? Because you have projected it out of yourselves. Being in God you are the producers of all phenomena, and you get entangled in the phenomena. Baidul says, 'We produce everything and become the slaves of that of which we are the masters.'

"When we breathe we don't pay attention to breathing; it is automatic, as in sound sleep. Breathing is our constant companion, but we do not pay attention to it. Just as we put on night clothes and go to sleep without paying attention to the clothes, and in the morning put off the night clothes and put on our day clothes without paying attention to them, except for a moment or two, so I am with you all the time, but you do not pay attention. How to pay attention, I may explain another time. You can not feel Me because I am there all the time; I will show you how to feel Me all the time.

"Let us have music. Indian music is all about love. Some of you may not like it, but I will explain it. I never question about God. I put questions to you about your health and food, but never about God, for I know I am God."

Francis says he has a million questions. Baba smiles.

After the first record, Baba says: "This is a wonderful state of love. The lover is not concerned with the planes and the different states of consciousness. He is only concerned with God and how to love God. He arrives at a stage when this love fills his world, and the pangs of separation are so unbearable that he says, 'I now want to forget You; but the more I try the more I remember You.' This torture is unbearable."

Baba proceeded to give interpretations of the words sung in the different records:

"Oh my beloved God, only he is fortunate and big-hearted who can not avoid shedding tears in his love. Oh you, who are training to be lovers of God, beware; you will be shown innumerable supernatural sights of different kinds; beware: only love God and do not be ensnared by these visions and powers.

"Oh you, who love to talk of love, do you know the difficulties and hardships facing you? The Master tests you at every step on the Path of Love."

Baba asked all to say whether they liked the music. Nearly everyone said he liked it and was much moved by the music. Purdom was alone in saying that he disliked it. "The majority has it," said Baba. "Don't talk to Me about music," He went on. "The first song I sang has brought the burden of all this universe upon Me."

He went on to say, "God is eternal; illusion semi-eternal. God does not change; illusion changes. Your shadow is always with you, but it changes in the morning from what it is later, and at midday you do not see it; the shadow is semi-eternal."

Malcolm asked, "Does God enjoy illusion?" Baba replied, "God as God-man enjoys illusion, but is free from it, for He governs illusion."

He said to Malcolm: "All these are words but words based on experience; you have that solace at least." Malcolm replied, "We should have more solace if you gave us the experience." Baba did not answer. The records and the interpretations continued:

"Here the Sufi of Experience says: Oh you, who have arrived at the Goal and know the secret of God, see that you reveal the secret only to the few select ones."

Baba said, "When Mansoor said 'I am God,' the Moslems got infuriated and hanged him."

"Oh Mansoor, even if you are hanged for having said you are one with Beloved God, do not reveal the secret. Oh Shams-i-Tabriz, because you raised the dead and the Moslems skinned you alive, do not reveal the secret.

"Oh Lovers of God, do not let what is in your hearts come to your lips.

"Remember, one who really loves God, God annihilates him; God mixes him with the dust."

Baba said, "And this was true of the Apostles of Christ and the Saviours."

"O Lover, beware, God tests you by being cruel, by giving you false hopes, even by cutting you to pieces."

"Kalyan says: 'The Master ties you fully dressed, hands and feet, onto a plank, throws you in mid-ocean, and says, if you love Me, let not one drop of water touch your clothes.' Why does he do this?" asked Baba. "The answer is that which Peter the chief Apostle was told, 'You will deny Me.' Why? Jesus said it and had it done. Why? Jesus, in that way, took the whole burden of the world and made Peter share it. To love means to lose your whole self with all its paraphernalia: it means torture, pangs, longing, and if despite all this, one is firm in his love, he becomes one with the Beloved. What was the height of suffering to Peter? That he denied his beloved Master! This denial was to enable him to share the sufferings of Jesus."

"The lover says that 'now the effect of your love has so infinitely widened my vision that wherever I go, I see nothing but you.

" 'I know, Beloved, I shall not be able to bear your glory. Yet I am ready to die; show me your face.' "

Baba went on to talk about Sanskrit and Persian. He said, "Try all of you to keep your lips tight and to say something. The sound will be *OM*. That is the seventh shadow of That Word. The Sanskrit language is based on *OM*. I personally prefer Persian."

He said of another record: "Some of you may like the

singer's voice, others may not. She is the greatest Indian *Qawaali* singer. She always sings about lovers of God. Here she sings about *masts* who, in love for God, have discarded everything and appear as mad. The *mast* says to the Beloved:

"If you want to make me mad for you, do so; but don't make me a laughing-stock. Oh you people of the world, who think me mad, and throw stones at me, if you were fortunate enough to have this love, you also would be mad like me.

"Oh you, who talk of loving God, you have to bow down to Him as though at every step, every particle of dust were a threshold to the Beloved."

A Persian record of Hafiz's poem was played, and Baba interpreted:

"Do not procrastinate. Start to love from this very moment. Do not forget the Beloved even for one instant."

Baba explained that the Master of Hafiz, whose name was Fariduddin Attar, had long tresses of black hair. Hafiz says in the following poem:

"Do not let your hair flow freely as my heart receives an arrow from every hair."

At the end he says:

"O Beloved! These tears that I shed are tears of blood so precious that you should consider them as pearls and wear them as earrings.

"God says, O Lover of Mine, if you want to enter My Lane (Path), first let your head roll under My feet and be kicked by Me as a ball.

"He says: I have been killed by your Love, and yet you cruel Beloved, you do not even glance at me."

Baba said: "So today we have tried to love God, we talked of love and heard songs of love. I am the most busy in the world. I have to look after the details of these meetings, and work on all planes. Yet I am the most inactive one.

Today we resolve that we must love God at any cost, and the most practical way to do it I will tell you at the meeting."

Baba was present during luncheon. He saw a number of the party, and then left, walking down the hill.

Monday, September 20

The members of the group were instructed to get up at 5 a.m. and be ready to leave before 7. We were at Ahmednagar at 7, where we met Baba and some of the Mandali. We set off for Sakori.

The cars stopped for a time at Rahuri, where Baba once had a *mast* ashram. Hundreds of people were there to meet Him and He walked through the town. It is a busy-looking town, a center of sugar-growing, with three sugar factories. The Mandali arrive on the top of a bus as their own small bus had broken down. Baba had said they would not arrive until evening.

Sakori was reached at 9:35. There was a large gathering of villagers to meet Baba, with a band of cymbals and drums from the ashram, also the town band with brass instruments and a banner. A white pony and a small donkey, both richly caparisoned, were there. The party was conducted to the ashram, led by the bands. The ashram was founded by Upasni Maharaj and contains His tomb. The place was scrub and a cremation ground; but it now contains extensive buildings where men and women live and work who have devoted their lives to Maharaj's work. There is a dairy with a fine herd of cattle. All the ashram have to work; the pony and donkey draw the water. The head of the ashram is Godavri, a small, sweet, serious, but sometimes smiling woman.

Baba was garlanded, and brought the group first to the women's quarters, then to the shrine and temple, the dairy and other buildings. He insisted that we should all be near Him wherever He went. There was a large crowd of people all the time.

Baba said, "This old man was God incarnate. I said at My last visit here that I would not again stop in Sakori. But I remembered that He had once said that visitors would come here from other lands to do devotion, and to fulfil this I had to come and bring you dear ones here. Now My work here is finished. After the meetings of the 29th and 30th, the following three months will be for My final work, to break My silence, to manifest, and then to die a violent death, all in quick succession. You should all bow down at Maharaj's *Samadhi*.* I am the Ancient One. When he threw *that stone* at Me, I knew I was the Ancient One."

"When He threw that stone *at Me, I knew I was the Ancient One"*

What Baba said first in English was translated into Marathi. *Arti* was sung by the women, which included a dwarf woman. Baba said, "You all can have no idea how

*Tomb

happy I am here. Godavri is the Mother here and all are her companions. She met Maharaj when two and a half years old; He put her on His lap and said, 'All this belongs to you.' They all live a life dedicated to My Master. I love her most dearly. The nuns are dressed in yellow saris and the candidates in white."

Bhajan sung by the women at Sakori

The Master tells His disciples that 'My Name is God
Some call Me Ram and some Shyam (Krishna)
In the world I am the object of worship and I am also the worshipper
At times I am the Giver and at times I am the beggar
I am everywhere and yet I belong to no place.'

(translated freely by Nariman Dadachanji, September 25, 1954)

With Godavri at Upasni Maharaj's tomb

Upasni Maharaj was a tall, heavy man and usually was naked, except for a gunny cloth and sandals when going out. For His last fourteen months and twelve days, He lived in a bamboo cage and took nothing but coffee once a day. The cage was about 3′ x 3 1/2′ so that he could not lie down. He died in a room shown to us. On a stone over the doorway to the room there is engraved Maharaj's will. The room contains the couch on which He died.

Baba paid His homage to the tomb, and one after another the members of the group did the same under Baba's guidance, kneeling down and kissing the stone.

The Mandali and others were given food in a lower room where Baba sat with them for a few minutes; then the group was taken to an upper room and given refreshments at small tables. The food was very tasty and daintily served. Baba sat there in a playful mood and threw the fruit from His table to be caught by various people. He barely touched His own food. He looked strained and suffering, as He did throughout the visit. A hymn was sung in His praise. At the end He said, "To find Me, you have to lose yourself. But these are just words when spoken and heard. Losing oneself and finding oneself is for very few lovers who carry their lives in their sleeves."

Baba visited a sick girl and fed her rose petals. He took the group to the ladies' dormitory and sat in a *jhula* or swing, and a girl sang the song Baba composed for Maharaj. The buildings were visited again with Baba. He sat with us in the temple and showed us Sai Baba's stick and pipe, kept in silver cases. It had been intended that we should visit Sai Baba's shrine at Shirdi, but there was no time.

On the way back, Baba stopped and got out of His car to inquire about Fred Marks, who had hit his head on a low doorway and had been bound up by Baba. Baba's attention was drawn by Dana Field to the danger of Baba wearing His scarf in His car, and Baba immediately removed it. He had lost His look of suffering.

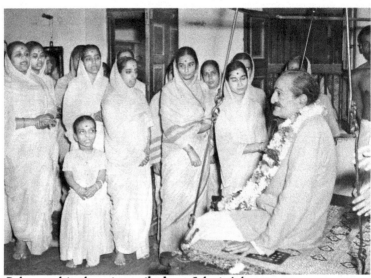

Baba seated in the swing or jhula *at Sakori Ashram*

Tuesday, September 21

Baba arrives at 10:15, having walked up the hill. He says He will stay longer today. Having inquired from each about his health, He says that He Himself is tired; He has not slept for three nights. He feels the burden of the universe. "I promised to teach you how to play marbles," He said. "I am above promises, but I have been reminded, and will do so." He explained that there are two types of games, showed us what they are and played one with us. We went into the lounge, and although the couch had been prepared with a rug and flowers He did not sit on it but took a chair in the corner of the room. He said He would first explain about Sakori, where He took us yesterday, and would talk as the thoughts came to Him, not necessarily consecutively. Later, He would speak about the 4th, 5th, 6th and 7th planes.

"First," He said, "about miracles, and why I think that

from the spiritual point of view, they are nothing but farce. When Jesus said, 'I and My Father are One,' He meant that He was God. Is this true? Did He actually say it? God created this entire phenomenal universe. That is God's miracle and the miracle of Jesus. It means that innumerable beings were created by Jesus who die according to His Will. Yet it is supposed that Jesus' greatness is that He raised some few dead to life. How ridiculous that is unless given some hidden meaning. It is supposed that He is the Savior because He raised a few dead and gave sight to the blind, creating insignificant illusions in the midst of His great illusion. Why is He supposed to have performed these miracles?"

Malcolm answered, "Because people were impressed by it."

"Yet," said Baba, "He said I am God, I am the Saviour, I am everything; but they were not impressed by that. If He raised the dead, people were impressed, which would mean that they were impressed not by Himself but by His so-called miracles. What do you say, Charles?"

Charles says that Jesus did not do these things to impress people because He told them to say nothing about them; whatever He did was because of His love. Baba went on to say that had Jesus not raised the dead, had He not performed the miracles, He would not have been crucified, and He wanted to be crucified. He performed the miracles to make certain of being crucified.

"Many miracles have been attributed to Me," Baba said, "but I do not perform miracles. I do not attach importance to miracles. When people think miracles have been performed, their faith has done it. One miracle I will perform, and for that miracle the time is nigh. I have said that My miracle will be not to raise the dead, but to make one dead to himself to live in God. I have repeatedly said I will not give sight to the blind, but I will make them blind to the world in order to see God.

"Why have I explained about miracles? It has to do

with Sakori. Yesterday we did not have time to go to Shirdi. There you would have found a different atmosphere from what exists at Sakori. People come there from all parts of India for Sai Baba's shrine. In almost every house in India, you will find Sai Baba's picture; it is in cinemas and on match boxes. This Divine Being is being commercialized...Sai Baba was Perfection personified, and the state of affairs at Shirdi I do not like. Soon I will change the whole atmosphere there....

"When I was in that superconscious state (it is called superconscious, which sounds foreign to Me, rather like the 'Superman'), this consciousness was of God. In that state, I was drawn to Shirdi near Sai Baba. When Sai Baba wanted to move His bowels, people would take Him in procession with a band and pipes. He was worthy of all that. He might stay there for an hour and the procession and band would return with Him to His seat. The first day I was drawn there, I had bloodshot eyes, and had had no sleep for days; and I laid down My head on His feet as He was walking in procession. He cried loudly, *'Parvardigar!'* meaning, 'You are God!' After saying that, He pointed in the direction where Upasni Maharaj sat.

"I went to Upasni Maharaj where He sat, thin and weak, and as soon as He saw Me, He picked up a stone and hit Me on the forehead, and instantaneously I recovered normal consciousness. Then I went with Him to Sakori, and stayed for seven years. Sakori was not then as you saw it. It was still wasteland, with a small hut for Upasni Maharaj. There was a woman there, an old lady called Durgamai, who loved Maharaj and Myself equally. People gathered there, mostly Brahmins, for Maharaj was Brahmin by birth.

"Shall I stop now and go on to the planes?" The answer was "No."

"It is all the same to Me," said Baba. "Who was the Master of Jesus? John the Baptist. You must have read how the disciples of John found fault with Jesus' disciples for living in comfort and having good food, when they had nothing of the kind. I will tell you how history repeats itself. Do not worry, do not doubt. God knows I am consciously One with Him. Yesterday a very peculiar thing happened. The president of a society in the south of India wrote Me to send a *mantra** there. They wanted Me to send a *mantra*, as they were preserving *mantras* and wanted something from My hand. They sent a new copybook for Me to fill. I dictated: 'I Am the Highest of the High: I Am the Ancient One.' I signed this with My own hand when written in the book."

Eruch said that this was the first time Baba had signed such a declaration with His own hand. Eruch had asked for a copy signed by Baba, for the office, which He gave.

"Why not say what I really am?" said Baba. "Divine honesty demands it."

"John the Baptist was a wonderful being. He gave his neck; he was the Master of Jesus. Jesus got Himself crucified. Last night I died a million deaths, and this morning I was so heavy in the head I thought of cancelling My visit to you. But suddenly I was well."

Baba resumed about Upasni Maharaj. "People began to come pouring in for His darshan, mostly Brahmins. A structure was erected and a Brahmin atmosphere prevailed. Maharaj and I used to sit together every day, and the Brahmins got jealous. 'Why is this Zoroastrian so favored by Maharaj?' they asked. Maharaj gradually gave hints of My divinity. Few could swallow this, many resented it, but our daily sittings continued. They built a Hindu temple there and performed the usual ceremonies. Then one day Maharaj declared to all the Mandali that Merwan is now Perfect."

Ramjoo, Adi Sr., and others were there at that period. Ramjoo said to us that the impression made on their minds was that Maharaj wanted them to follow Baba and to carry

*Sentence for meditation

out His orders, important or unimportant, even though they found them difficult. Adi said, "He wanted us to stick to Baba through thick and thin." Ramjoo said that Maharaj declared He had given up everything to Baba; He had handed Him the "key."

"From that day," continued Baba, "I did not go to Sakori. And from that time the Hindu atmosphere increased. Maharaj encouraged them to be jealous of Me, and to be bitter, and to hurt Me. But Maharaj told Durgamai and Yeshwantrao that Merwan is now 'Malik'* of the Universe. When the Brahmins heard Me called 'Malik,' they wanted to kill Me. We were both unaffected by all this.

..."Then Godavri came; and Maharaj said, 'I do not want this Brahmin atmosphere of men,' and He began to gather girls of pure character who wanted to love God only. The novices are dressed in white and are called *Kanyas*.

"Later on Maharaj sent word by Adi's mother Gulmai, 'Soon I will drop this body, so tell Merwan to come to see Me.' I said I would not set foot in Sakori, so a meeting was arranged elsewhere in a hut.** We embraced each other and I put My head under His foot. He said, 'You are *Adishakti*.'† Again He started weeping, and said to Me, 'Keep your eye on Sakori.' Then we both went away, and three to four months later, Maharaj dropped His body, and Godavri was given charge of the nuns. Godavri was in the secret all the time, but never said a word about me. But the atmosphere there was Hindu, with their ceremonies. I have come to destroy in the world all rites and ceremonies that are superficial. Godavri loved Me in secret. The men there made it appear that I was not the spiritual heir of

*Owner

**Described in the Nov., 1941, issue of *The Meher Baba Journal; Awakener*, Vol. 14, 3-4

†The Supreme Power

Maharaj, only of Babajan, and spread the news that Godavri was in charge of the ashram and Maharaj's spiritual heir. Poor girl, she is so good, a wonderful soul among women. She was in a fix, but her good nature kept her going.

"Then My disciples increased and the Sakori Brahmins got more and more annoyed, like the disciples of John the Baptist. Then a miracle happened. . .all due to Godavri. Her loving influence overcame the Brahmin atmosphere. She at last saw Me at 'Nagar and asked Me to come once to Sakori. As I had promised Maharaj I would keep an eye on Sakori, I took the occasion of Yeshwantrao's house-warming to go.

"Godavri welcomed Me, placed her head on My feet, garlanded Me, and placed Me on the swing where Maharaj used to sit. . .I embraced all the group and they all melted. Godavri showed her love so clearly that the entire atmosphere cleared. As you saw at the *darshan* on the 12th of September, Godavri and the men were there. Now they all love Me and recognize Me as the Avatar.

"I want you to understand, however, that the miracle atmosphere is still at Sakori, though not so much as at Shirdi...People try to raise the status of Maharaj by these petty things. They have good intentions, but I will put an end to all this. God, Love, Truth and Purity are free from all these absurdities, and free most of all from rituals and ceremonies, done without heart or understanding, only because of custom."

Baba then took his seat on the couch. He said, "Rest for five minutes." He talked about other matters. He then said, "Do you want me to go on about planes?" The answer from a number was, "Yes." He then drew some lines on paper and got Eruch to write some letters on it. "This is something new," He said.

Baba went on: "Continuing our discussion from the day before yesterday: the soul now goes to the fourth plane of consciousness. This is known as the junction between the subtle and the mental planes. It is also called *Asthana*, meaning 'threshold.' Here there is no *manzil*, no *muqam*. It is the junction where the infinite energy, the desires, emotions and feelings of the mental plane are the direct influence. The soul is now neither on the subtle nor on the mental plane, but all the powers of the subtle and all of the influences of the mental plane are continually with it. There is no *manzil*. The soul is now so overpowered by desires and by its ability to satisfy its desires that it is in danger of falling from the spiritual heights to the lowest depths. It can now do anything, raise the dead, create new forms, do anything it wants. Desires influence it with all their force: it is in great danger. The details are in *God Speaks*.

"If the soul does not then succumb to the use of its infinite energy for selfish ends, it reaches the fifth plane and the fifth *manzil*. As I said, in the gross world there is the first *manzil* with its innumerable *muqams*. In the first plane of the subtle are the second *manzil* and its *muqams;* in the second plane of the subtle, the third *manzil* and its *muqams;* in the third plane of the subtle, the fourth *manzil* and its *muqams;* in the fourth plane no *manzil* and no *muqam*.

"In the fifth plane, which is in the mental sphere, there are the fifth *manzil* and its *muqams*. What happens in this fifth state? The soul is now working directly from the mental plane. Is this clear? The soul is master of the mind: the entire mental plane is governed by it. It knows the thoughts and desires of everyone, but is safe, as the 'dark night' of the fourth plane has been passed. Remember I am skipping over these matters. The soul now knows the thoughts and desires, but cannot control the desires. On this fifth plane, it cannot have that intense longing for God which lovers who do not know or care about planes have. When it progresses to the sixth plane, which includes the second function of mind, the soul *becomes* feelings, desires, emotions personified; and as all infinite feelings come from God, Who is the seventh state of consciousness, the soul now directly sees God everywhere and in everything, yet feels itself aloof from the Beloved. Here there is the great abyss, beyond which the lover sees the Beloved, and feels separated from the Beloved. The Beloved says, 'Come to Me.' The lover says, 'I cannot: You come to me!' This glorious state is described as one end of a hair in the hand of the Beloved and the other in that of the lover; there is a long tussle. If the Beloved pulls too hard, the hair will break; so the tussle goes on for years and years. Among millions of such lovers of God who long for union with God, one will reach the Beloved. Very, very few lovers succeed. When one crosses the valley and is united with God, he finds that it was himself he was seeking. He, himself, is the Beloved. He then knows, 'I am God.' Of thousands of such united ones, one comes down to normal consciousness, and is called *Qutub*, or Christ, or Avatar, or Perfect Master .

"The sixth plane has a *manzil* and one *muqam*, God, whom the soul sees everywhere. I talk of God and you go to God in sound sleep!*

"Now let us look at the diagram. There are seven planes, seven *manzils,* innumerable *muqams* in six planes, one *muqam* in the gross sphere, and one *muqam* in the sixth *manzil*. In the fourth plane there is no *manzil* and no *muqam*.

"When you remember Me, you are in *Sahaj Dhyan*. The question is how to remember Me. The easiest and surest way is to do as I tell you. It will be somewhat of a task at first, as when you start to run you feel it too much; but when you are in training, you feel it *sahaj*.** At first you will have to do it deliberately, then it will become natural. There are four quarters of the day and there are four divisions in man's physical state: childhood, youth, maturity, old age. There are four quarters that Kabir calls the signposts. The first thing in the morning when you get

*A disciple had fallen asleep.
**Naturally.

up, before doing anything, think for one second of Baba. Baba is then worn by your soul: early in the morning dress your soul with Baba. At 12 noon, for one second, do the same; do it again about 5 o'clock; when you retire do it also. I have never asked anyone to do this, not even the Mandali. If you do it I will be always with you, and you will feel My company all the time. Do it for four seconds every day, then you will be in the world, yet Baba will be with you all the time. This is the beginning of *Sahaj Dhyan.*

"Sitting in the swing *(jhula)* is derived from Krishna. His mother rocked Him in a cradle. The *Gopis* made Him sit on a swing. It is now customary for Perfect Masters to sit so. This is not to keep them awake, but is a sort of lullaby: 'Krishna, now sleep and don't make trouble' — that is what is meant. Krishna was very mischievous, full of practical jokes, and used to make trouble. Christ and Buddha had other ways. I think I am a mixture of all.

"Babajan was active and had bright eyes, and even at the age of 125 She was extremely active. She always sat under the tree, rain or shine. You could feel love flowing freely from Her. She once told the group there, 'I have so made this Son of Mine that one day He will make the whole world dance around His fingers.' There was no talk of money then, people just came for darshan. If anyone asked for anything, She got out a stick. Always She stroked Her left arm. I can't explain why, but She did it purposely. She used to walk fast, and at 85 She would run fast. Years ago the Mandali had to run or use their bicycles to keep up with Me. She gave Me divine bliss; Sai Baba gave Me divine power; Upasni Maharaj gave Me divine knowledge.

"To sum up, we have to feel in our heart of hearts that only God is real, that He alone exists, that He is in us all, that He alone is to be loved: God and God alone.

"From now on there are to be no sittings at night for the young men, and no more morning meditations for anyone. On the 24th, at 12 midnight, everyone is to keep awake and think of Me for half an hour. Do this with all your hearts. All of you, or at least one of you, will see Me: I am there. Seeing Me means a picture of Me a long way off. Keep My form before your mind's eye. The eyes may be open or shut, but keep Me before your mind."

He asked us to sit for one minute with our eyes closed, and to picture Him after first looking at Him. Afterwards He asked what happened. Francis said, "It comes and goes." Baba replied, "Because you come and go! I am there always."

"Do you know how St. Francis loved Jesus and became one with Him? He loved Him as Jesus ought to be loved; but in Francis' group there was one who was a glutton. Juniper loved Francis most, though he did not sit in meditation or think of anything. He gave more trouble to Francis than anyone, yet he loved Francis dearly. When we love from the bottom of our hearts we give all our good and bad, even our trouble; the lover gives everything and demands nothing. I give everything and demand nothing in return. Love me like that and Baba is your slave. Even if you can't do that, don't worry. As long as you are Mine, you need not worry. You are Mine, that is why I have drawn you such long distances. If you can't picture Me, don't worry; if you don't love Me, don't worry: I love you. At midnight on the 24th, don't force, be natural, keep calm; don't sit like Yogis.

"It is said of Me that I am most slippery.

"Now, one secret. Try to picture your wife and child: in an instant they are here. This is of no great importance, but it helps a little. You can bring them from Australia, but you can't bring Baba from here."

Wednesday, September 22

Baba arrived at 10:30 a.m. He did not walk up the hill, and appeared to be very strained and tired. He went at once into the lounge, after greeting everyone. He said, "Today there is nothing to explain. I did not feel like coming today. Yet I wanted to see you dear ones, so I decided to come. I have much to think about before the meetings. My thinking is not just thinking: the whole burden is upon Me."

He inquired about the health of each individual, as usual. "You must all be fit for the two days of the meeting. Dear Will," He went on, "I call you My archangel, and you are very devoted to Me, and I love you intensely; but I can not understand your saying every day 'I am better today.'" Will explains it means he sleeps better every night. To others Baba said, "I do not believe you when you say you are very well."

"I used to say to the Mandali," said Baba, "that in God's work Maya always opposes: it is necessary. Just as illusion is necessary for the realization of God, so Maya's force in opposing God's work gives strength to the work. The greater the opposition from Maya, the better the result.

"Before the Mass Darshan on the 12th, Ahmednagar had had a record rainfall. Sarosh came to Me to say that if the rain did not stop, the *darshan* would have to be postponed. I said, what God wants will happen. When the weather changed, it was thought to be Baba's miracle! That is absolute nonsense. I do not say this to display humility: it is a fact. I said that I did not mind the rain. God may want rain, but the meeting will be held. If it rains, they will get wet, they will have to change, and I will have to change. The meetings on the 29th and 30th will be the first and last meetings of the kind. As the day approaches for these meetings the burden is lowering on My head, just as the clouds lower in the sky. If you don't keep your health it will be an additional burden." Baba goes on to give advice and orders.

"I sometimes seem to be speaking at random, but I am really working elsewhere.

"When you say 'I am ill, I am hungry, I am old, I am young, or I am not hungry and do not want this food' and so on, when you use all these I, I, I's, recollect that when your hands or legs are cut off, your 'I' remains the same; whatever happens you remain the same. This means that the 'I' is not the body. Why identify yourself with the body? Yet for 24 hours a day you do so. Will used to say, 'I am thirsty.' He now says in old age, 'I am better.' If that were true it would mean that Will was the same limited body.

" '*Aham*' means identification with the false. Why do we do this? Even when we understand, we still identify. Why? The 'I' is not the body, nor the eating nor the quarreling one. For ages the unlimited Self has been in illusion, because consciousness and intellect were not developed. In the human form consciousness and intellect are developed, but there is identification with illusion because of the habits of ages. Hafiz says: 'You, who do not come out of this age-long habit of being ignorant, can never realize the Self as infinite.'

"It is truly said that God has no beginning and no end. Think this over. If He had no beginning, what was there before God? The answer is, God. You cannot in imagination reach where no beginning was. The answer can only be God. What will be there after billions of years? God. Always God. This means that in Eternity there is no time. Nothing has ever happened, and nothing ever will happen. There is no time factor. Billions of years ago you were: today you are here, ever afterwards you will be. Today all that is happening is not happening, though this does not appear to be so now.

"When one has experience of Eternity, one knows that God is. To say that God was, is and will be, is wrong. All Eternity is now present at this moment. So I say, 'God is.'

"Mona* was once here with you; she is no longer with you. The meaning is that she never was here with you; she always was in Eternity. Even I cannot express this, but I

*The wife of Malcolm Schloss, who died in 1954.

try to do so as far as possible. It is beyond the intellect. What happened yesterday has produced a temporary effect; but the actual happening of yesterday has stopped, which means that nothing happened yesterday. The temporary effect is illusion. So it goes on: God and illusion running parallel. Illusion says everything is happening, God says nothing happens.

"When you are in the grip of the false 'I,' which identifies itself with what happens, illusion governs you. But when you know the truth, you do not identify yourself with it. All we see, hear and experience in the world is not God. Whatever you can understand, is not God. Whatever is explained is not God. Whatever is expressed is not God. The poet says:

" 'The lover says to the Master: You have taught me something that has made me forget everything. You have created in me a desire that says, do not desire anything. You have given me that One Word which says, words mean nothing.

" 'And the lover says: Oh Master, I was seeking God and thought Him this and that. Now you have given me something of which even my imagination cannot produce the shadow.'

"It is all words. When you say Self, God, Infinity, they mean nothing. To attempt to understand by reading or hearing explanations is an insult to our beloved God, Who is beyond all understanding. The only answer is Love. If we love God, we become Him. There is no further question. But we must love with all our hearts, so that only God exists for us."

There followed some music. Then Ben Hayman came in and Baba welcomed him and asked him if he slept well, and said He was very happy to see him. "I wanted you here, so you came." He told him to relax, and said that He wanted him to feel that he had not missed anything.

"There will be no more explanations. I will play marbles with you! I am so full of humor and so human that it is difficult even for *Rishis*† and Saints to know Me as I am. I am at every level and act according to that level. With a child I am a child; with the highest saints I am one with them. It is My nature to be absolutely natural, even with beloved God, Who is one with Me, and I with Him.

"If you understand what I have just said, the solution to everything is in your hands. God is infinite honesty, and unless we love Him honestly we can not know Him. Though beyond understanding, the heart full of love can understand the un-understandable. If you love God you become one with Him; that is the only thing. And you *can* love God."

Malcolm asked if we weren't really loving God whenever we loved anyone or anything. Baba said, "Yes. Only you don't know that you are loving God: God loves Himself through us all.

"When I washed the feet of the seven poor, and bowed down to them, I did it with all My heart. I did not merely play the part of one who bows down and gives gifts: I became *that*. What did you see that day? This bowing down is due to Perfect Ones, according to Hindu custom, also the giving of gifts. I became by My act, the devotee and disciple of seven Perfect Ones. I placed My head on their feet and gave gifts. I am everything, but I became all this, and honesty demands that what I am, I must express."

Thursday, September 23

Baba arrives at 9:30, goes at once to the lounge. Inquires about health. All must be fit by the 29th and 30th. The wind is not good for throats: keep warm.

"All explanations are stopped from today. Tomorrow I will take you all to the village. I love these poor people of Arangaon. Tomorrow at a quarter to four the villagers want to do *Arti*, and I have permitted them. The village is

†Advanced souls

full of germs, but with Me everything is safe because I am the poorest of the poor. I say that and really am that: emperor and beggar at one and the same time.

"This reminds Me that from the day I stopped speaking, I stopped touching money. I don't touch money, but it comes and goes. Disciples from the East and the West give money, but I touch money only when I give to the *masts* and to the poor people on special occasions. I then take money in My hand to give them. Sometimes I have distributed grains. But the important thing is that I must wash their feet and bow down before handing over the gift. As I told you yesterday, I do not only play the part but become *that*. You must have heard and read years back that there were a dispensary, a hospital, an ashram for the boys, a leper asylum and a *mast* asylum for the God-mad. I supervised the boys, lepers, *masts*, and washed their clothes, cleaned their latrines; not for show or humility, but I became *that*. The people of this village are very dear to Me. You will see how they live in mud houses. I say this because yesterday Frank and Ben were seen going towards the village, and I sent a message that they were not to go. You must be fit for the 29th and 30th. But I thought these men, women and children are dear to Me and why not let you see them? I have no time Myself nowadays even to take a bath; I have not had My hair washed for three months. I have no time and no sleep.

"At the meetings, people are coming from all parts of India and Pakistan who love Me. This is My last meeting, and I want to say some things that will last till I come back in 700 years. So be fit and in the mood to listen.

"Maharaj had told Yeshwantrao that Merwan is *Parabrahman,* which means 'God beyond.' 'So do whatever Merwan tells you to do,' He said. As I told you I did not sleep for nine months. Then I was with Maharaj till one or two o'clock in the night, and went to a small hut nearby and Yeshwantrao was there with Me. He would press My feet and give Me betel leaves. I did not eat, but every five minutes asked for 'pan' (betel leaves). He could not sleep because I did not sleep. For seven years this man served Me with such love as is rarely found. When the atmosphere that I have described existed, it was Yeshwantrao who was the target of these Brahmins for attending Me. But Yeshwantrao was adamant. He obeyed Maharaj by obeying Me, so he was put to great suffering, physically and mentally. Now the atmosphere is clear. He does not remind anyone of the old days. It is as if he has forgotten everything. He helps them with corn and money. Yeshwantrao has now Maharaj and Baba as one in his heart. The refreshments you had there were provided by his help.

"We are all meant to be as honest as God, as loving as God, as happy as God: and only the Christ suffers for humanity, although He is the source of all happiness. You see Me in this physical form, but every moment I am crucified. Only those fortunate ones know this. I suffer as no one could suffer; I suffer because I love. Godavri is one of the most lovable beings in the world, and what she has tried to do all these years!

"How Godavri loves Me and what a virgin she is! She is like Krishna's mother. Sometime ago a well-known astrologer came to pay homage to Maharaj. I had already sent news to the West and elsewhere that I should break My silence and meet a violent death. She had had that circular and was much depressed. The date and time of My birth were given to the astrologer; and he said the months of November and December would be very hard for Me. They asked for some relief for Me. This man said that for fifteen days there should be ceremonies and mantras for Baba to relieve Him from this suffering. This was done of their own accord. A letter from the chief priest of the temple said this had happened, and that they willingly and lovingly performed the ceremonies, and kept the ashes according to their custom. I followed out what they wanted because of their great love. Nothing can stop what has to happen. I have to break My silence before the end of the year, to manifest, and to drop this body. What is ordained must be. If people love God as I want them to do, My work is accomplished.

"Were there any other promises?" Baba asked. Malcolm said, "To talk about repression?" Baba said, "In a few words I will tell you about repression.

"Illusion is a temporary phenomenon: something that is not what it appears to be. On this are based the following words: Illusion creates innumerable illusions, and each illusion leaves the marks of experience in the form of impressions. For example, during the night, you are asleep and on waking up, your hand touches something near the bed and at once you think it is a scorpion. You have created a scorpion which is not there. But you shrink with fear, get out of bed, get a stick and hit the supposed scorpion. Then you see it was not a scorpion but something else. Though there was no scorpion, the impressions of getting frightened, getting out of bed and hitting the scorpion are now stamped on your mind, and somehow have to be spent. So illusion continues, gaining impressions and spending impressions, and all the time illusion is preserved.

"Once in Meherabad, down the hill, when there was the big colony and I had dissolved it all and moved to a new place named Toka, a few miles away, a few were kept here. An Irani who was good in heart, but a bit 'cracked,' had to keep guard at night. He had to shout out at intervals 'All's well,' to keep himself awake as well as to show others that he was awake. At that time there was a very notorious thief who had robbed and killed a number of people, called Satyamang. One night this man had robbed a man on the road from here to Ahmednagar. The following night something happened to this dear man (Irani): a donkey wandered here and he thought it was Satyamang! So he awakened everyone and all were nervous. One old Mandali fainted. All the time the man was shouting 'Satyamang is here!' After a time a lantern was lighted and it was seen there was nobody there; then the door was opened and the donkey was seen.

"When I heard this story I thought this illusion beats even the universal illusion I created ages ago! Then I sent for Satyamang, who was so proud of his strength that the police feared him and the villagers were afraid to report his threats. 'I don't know Baba, get out,' he said to My messenger and he abused Me. But later on he came, saying he had seen Baba in a dream sitting on his chest. I was sitting as usual, and as soon as he saw Me, Satyamang prostrated himself and started weeping. I called him and made him sit quietly by My side. 'I want you from today to give up robbing and killing and to disperse your gang, and for your living come to Me and I will supply you.' I said. He promised. From that day the man dropped his old ways. Once there was a lapse: after some months he thought of robbing someone. A money lender had left his house empty, and Satyamang was tempted to rob it. He broke in, and saw My form standing there in the doorway. So he came at once to Me and said, 'You have saved me.' When I went away to Persia and left only one family here, I told him to look after the place.

"At times I have plenty of money, at other times I have little or none. In the New Life, I begged food and made the Mandali beg. Satyamang had stopped robbing. He was living close by and he brought food to the family, begging from village to village for them. There were many other incidents attributed to Me as My miracles. Even now people say they see Me in My physical form. But I have not yet performed a single miracle. I know nothing about them. Their love and faith gives them the experience.

"When I break My silence I will perform the greatest of miracles — My first and last miracle in this Incarnation of Mine. If people tell you Baba has performed this or that miracle, let the story go out of the other ear. My greatness does not lie in performing miracles. My greatness lies in

suffering for the universe, because I love all.
"Repressions: you work it out for yourself, Malcolm.
Let us play marbles!"

Baba's Arti

by Dana Field

The Call of Baba is God's Voice,
The Order of Baba is God's Will,
The Prasad of Baba is God's Substance,
The Darshan of Baba is God's Presence,
The Love of Baba is God's Grace,
The Goal of Baba is God-Realization.

Friday, September 24

Baba arrives at 10 a.m. on foot, pale and worn, but smiling.
"No more explanations today," he said. "It is the last
day of My coming here. Today we will drink together. This
is not the Last Supper, but the Last Drink, and I am happy
that at least from among you all no one will sell Me, though
someone has to do that job. My physical end is going to be a
violent one. I am the Ancient One, and you will all love Me
more and more after My body is dropped, and will see Me
as I really am. Today I won't explain anything; what is
there to explain?

"You all say, 'Yes Baba,' but do not do.

"My ways are so unfathomable that sometimes I too
can not fathom them."

He refers to the photographs. "This is not Baba. If you
had but a glimpse of Me as I am, you would lose
consciousness. Love me and you will be loving God. And
God is to be loved honestly. The slightest hypocrisy or
dishonesty keeps you far away from God. God our Beloved
is here now in you all, Who knows what you will think
tomorrow. He is all Knowledge, and when we love Him

honestly, He becomes one with us. It is not that we have to become one with Him, but He becomes one with us. My last message to you, dear ones, is to love God, and you will find I am one with God."

There was an interval for interviews.

On returning, Baba looked at a photograph of Himself as a young man and said, "I love Him very much."

Baba sent for the drinks. He said the poor have little food, and those at Assam and elsewhere suffer from the floods. "I am in all, and I am in Eternal Bliss, because of God, and in everlasting suffering, through these souls. I want to make people not only food-minded, but God-minded. That is why I have called these meetings.

"I am infinitely restless, and infinitely at peace simultaneously.

"Jesus, being God and omnipotent, allowed Himself to be helpless, humiliated and crucified. He knew it all, because He had planned it all, long ago, and He did it for all. But to have the right result, He had to experience the helplessness and the suffering. Do not think that because He was all-powerful, He did not suffer the humiliation and the crucifixion, or it would not then have had the desired effect. Some people think that because I am one with God, My body is not affected by anything. At times, so as not to hurt their feelings, I have to behave as though I do not feel cold or the sun. Someone came and sat by me when full of cold, and thought 'as Baba is God, this can not affect Him.' But I am on the human level, and must behave as on the human level. So when I saw she had cold and fever, I also saw that she would not like it if I turned away, so I held My breath. The first time I was in London, it was drizzling and cold, and everyone was wearing warm clothes, and they wanted Me to be filmed in these thin clothes, thinking it did not matter to Me. So I had to feel cheerful and I afterwards sent for a warm coat. All the Mandali know that when Meherabad was in full swing with asylums, hospitals, etc., I was very thin; and when I discarded the old coat of Mine, I used to go about supervising and being cheerful with everyone, and being everywhere, and used to keep fit. Even now I feel fit, but I think I shall catch cold from you all."

The fruit drinks were brought in and put before Baba, only the Westerners remaining, except Eruch. The doors were shut; there was silence. Baba said, "For one minute close your eyes and ask God, Who is the innermost Self of us all, to help us to love Him honestly." He then sipped from each glass, and handed a glass to each one. "Drink slowly," He said. When all had finished, the doors were opened, the Mandali came in and had a glass each, not sipped by Baba.

He got up and said, "Now we will all go to the dome." We visited the dome, the graves and Baba's room, and afterward Baba sat with us under a tree. Then He went down the hill, taking only an Indian boy with Him.

Friday, September 24 — Afternoon

At 2:30 p.m. on the afternoon of September 24th, Baba returned from the men's ashram and gathered us together for several group photographs which, as a group, we had requested permission to have taken with Him. A professional photographer from Ahmednagar was present, and photographs were taken in the field alongside the house, in front of Baba's tomb and alongside the tomb, in front of the little meditation cubicles which had been used by some of Baba's Mandali years ago, during one of His seclusions.

At 2:45 p.m. Baba led us all down the hill to the men's ashram, where we were joined by the Mandali living there, and a number of Baba's disciples and devotees from various parts of India. When we had all gathered about Baba in the large hall, Baba had Vishnu recite Upasni Maharaj's "Praise of the Ten Avatars." Then one of His devotees from Madras, M. Ramalinga Shastri, read in Sanskrit that

Westerners at Meherabad; standing, left to right: John Bass, Dr. Ben
Hayman, Charles Purdom, Fred Winterfeldt, Malcolm Schloss, Will Backett,
Frank Hendricks, Bill Le Page, Francis Brabazon, BABA (seated), John
Ballantyne, Joseph Harb, Fred Frey, Lud Dimpfl, Dana Field, (in front of Fred
Marks), Darwin Shaw, Philippe DuPuis, Frank Eaton, Dr. William
Donkin, Not present: Dr. Allan Chamberlin, Max Haefliger, Zandor
Markey, who also attended at various times.

passage from the Bhagavad Gita in which Krishna says: "Age after age, from time immemorial, for the destruction of ignorance, for the preservation of Truth, I have taken human form."

When he had finished Baba said,"You say this as if you were swimming in mid-ocean and attacked by sharks." Then Baba continued wryly, "I have created everything, and yet I don't know Sanskrit. I just nod My head as if I knew." Evidently He considers Persian, English, Hindi, Gujarati, Urdu and Marathi adequate to serve Him in this incarnation.

Baba then called another of His disciples from the ashram, Sidhu Kamble, and asked him to sing a devotional song, which Sidhu did with varied inflection and appropriate gestures, which Baba translated, at least in part, with occasional comments.

"One who loves," it ran, "can not talk about living, and my Beloved seems not to care for me. When my heart was drawn by the locks of my Beloved, I thought the locks were very near, but now I have walked all my life, until my feet are full of blisters, and they are still far from me."

Here Baba interjected, "Baba also is so near, and yet so far!"

Then the song continued. "When the lips of separation tried to touch the cup of Union, hundreds and hundreds of lovers were burned," at which Baba applauded.

After this He arose, and led us to the *Dhuni* nearby, where blocks and shavings of sandalwood had been heaped and covered with *ghee**, and about which a crowd of Arangaon villagers had gathered, waiting for Baba to light the *Dhuni* and begin the ceremonies which they had planned as a mark of their devotion to Him. Following the lighting of the *Dhuni* came the performance of *arti* by the headman of Arangaon and several women, who also

*Clarified butter.

garlanded Baba and took the dust of His feet. Then an elderly native with an elephant horn mounted the platform on which the *Dhuni* is situated, and was embraced warmly by Baba who invited him to blow the ancient horn.

This was apparently a signal for the procession from the *Dhuni* to the village to begin, and it was led by men dancers from the village, who performed a harvest dance to the accompaniment of drums, bells and chains, with an occasional blast from the elephant horn. All the way along the road from the *Dhuni* to the village, which is about a quarter of a mile, men, women and children who had been waiting by the *Dhuni* and at the edge of the road, pressed forward, trying to touch Baba and, if possible, to take the dust of His feet.

Arangaon is a sixteenth-century small walled town, now fallen into almost complete decay. It still contains evidence of the prosperity it once enjoyed, in the wood-carving and color-decoration surviving in the ruined temple and other buildings, for the countryside was then much more fertile than it is now. The present population of about 2,000 lives in the ruins. The Western Gateway still stands with the shrine of the Monkey God, the protector of the town, outside it.

Arriving at the village, we found throngs of men, women and children crowding the narrow streets in anticipation of Baba's visit. "*Avatar Meher Baba Maharaj ki jai!*" rose from their lips in a grand chorus of welcome, and they pressed forward to garland Baba and prostrate themselves at His feet. In no time He was covered with garlands of jasmine and roses, which he kept on for hours, in spite of the intense afternoon heat. He led us in turn through temples and houses, introducing us to various families of His devotees, including so-called "untouchables," with comments on their poverty, on His love for them, and on their devotion for Him, all of which were abundantly evident. He had said to us in the morning that He was giving us the "Last Drink" instead of the "Last

Supper." This procession through Arangaon village reminded some of us of Jesus walking through the Galilean villages with the people crowding upon Him, touching Him, and bringing their children to Him.

At every turn our hearts were warmed by simple, natural, spontaneous expressions of genuine love, both human and divine. It seemed as if a river of love were losing itself in an ocean of love, and only boundless love existed. Incident after incident occurred which touched us deeply. In one of the simple, crude houses into which Baba led us, a very old man prostrated himself full length on the dirt floor in front of Baba, sobbing with devotion. Baba lifted him gently, and embraced him. In the crowded streets, as Baba moved forward, followed by throngs of people, women set down their children at the side of the street and dashed out to touch His feet as He passed. One had a garland that she wanted to present, and desperately tried to reach Him without success, until He turned, stopped, and reached out His hand, and accepted it, moving swiftly on again.

After about an hour and a half of successive visiting, garlanding, and giving *darshan*, Baba gathered us around Him in a small enclosure, where three young girls danced for Him to the accompaniment of music from an harmonium, bells and drums. Following this, Baba gave *prasad* and *darshan* to about 200 people. Then the procession through the town was resumed, with Baba leading us into the quarters of the untouchables, and finally to the houses occupied by some of the families of the Mandali, where coconuts were broken at His feet, *darshan* was given, more garlands were placed around His neck.

At one point, referring to the untouchables, Baba remarked, "These poor people are ordinarily not allowed to move among the rest of society," to which Joseph Harb replied, "Well, it seems to me as if they were now moving in the best of society," meaning Baba's company, of course.

Everywhere we moved, in spite of Baba's pre-occupation with these deeply devoted villagers, His continuous solicitude for the welfare of the Western group was constantly made manifest. He would stop every once in a while to be sure that we were all close to Him. We were reminded to watch our heads while entering low doorways; we were not to stumble over piles of stones, or water-drains; and once Baba ordered a boy to stand on a tree-stump in the middle of the road so that we should not trip over it. There was no limit to His love or His solicitude, nor of His ability freely to express them.

At about six o'clock, Baba ordered us back to the men's ashram to wait for Him, while He went to visit the patients in a tuberculosis hospital nearby. When He returned, He gathered us about Him in the large hall and ordered us each to take two tablets of Anacin and quinine before retiring, as a precaution against malaria, some cases of which, He said, had arisen in the village. The He gave us each what He said would have to be His last personal embrace, as from that time He would be unable to see us privately again. It was the crowning moment of what will always be a gloriously memorable day.

Sunday, September 26

Baba decided several days ago to give *darshan* to those of Ahmednagar and the vicinity who had not been able to be present at the large darshan gathering of the 12th. A platform and a seat were accordingly erected in the patio of the Khushroo Quarters, where Adi Irani lives and where Meher Publication Office is, and alongside of which the Sarosh Motor Works is located. We were ordered to be present at 3:30 p.m., when the program was scheduled to begin.

When we arrived, there were crowds of men, women and children waiting outside the compound. We were led to Baba by Adi, and He embraced each of us in turn. Then

He seated Ben Hayman, Frank Hendricks and Charles Purdom alongside Him on the platform, and motioned for the rest of us to range ourselves about Him on the ground.

Ben Hayman, Meher Baba, Eruch, Charles Purdom

Ben and Frank had been delayed in coming to India, and had not seen the darshan on the 12th. Also on the platform back of Baba were Eruch, Mr. Jessawala, Krishna, Kaka, Kumar, Goolmai, Dr. P. Natrajan, John Spiers, and Bal Dhavale who had come to take motion pictures of the occasion.

Soon a stream of women in varicolored saris was flowing past Baba at the rate of 45 a minute, many of them leading or carrying children. All castes, creeds and religions were represented in the crowd, and all stages of material circumstances. At various times Baba sat on the seat, on the platform, on the step leading to the platform, and on the ground, and at least once He stood on the platform for a period of time.

Meher Baba at the "Little Darshan"

The women and children were followed by the men, old, middle-aged, and young, with varicolored turbans and flowing robes. At one time, Baba spelled out on His board, "No explanations or discourses can compare with this personal contact. I feel that I am in all. It is Baba bowing down to Baba."

Those who passed Him sometimes touched His feet

with their heads, sometimes with their hands. Some brought garlands, which they placed around His neck. Some, at intervals, were only allowed to fold their hands and bow before Him. Some brought money which they were not permitted to leave.

At one point, a poor woman placed a *pice,* a coin which, at the present rate of exchange, is worth about a third of a cent, on Baba's left foot. For a while, Baba left it there. It has been His custom, for many years, not to touch money. Later, He turned His foot, the coin fell off, He covered it with gravel, and sat for a long time in complete absorption, gazing at the spot where the coin lay. After a while, He stood up, still in His mood of abstraction. His eyes fixed on the gravel where the coin was buried. Baba had a very serious expression on His face. What He was thinking we could not know.

Occasionally Baba would give special attention to

Avatar Meher Baba gazes pensively at a coin by His foot

various children who passed Him in the line, drawing them to Him for a special embrace. Usually they were children with large, luminous eyes. Perhaps Baba saw in them future saints or Masters.

One old man in a red turban and a flowing white beard came back for a second *darshan*. The police wanted to move him on, but Baba held him and embraced him warmly, placing one of His garlands around his neck. Occasionally He would give a garland to some woman or child who passed. "I love them all," He said at one time, "big, small, high, low, rich, poor, all." And again, "I am whatever anyone takes Me to be."

At one time Baba motioned all of us to move out of the sun and sit closer to Him in the shade. At another time He called Frank Eaton and John Bass to sit beside Him, as they would then be more comfortable. Occasionally He would bend down, pick up a stone, and throw it to one of the Western group.

At a quarter to six, the queue of waiting people was still long, and Sarosh tried to persuade Baba to stay

A coin (one pice) on Baba's foot makes Him thoughtful

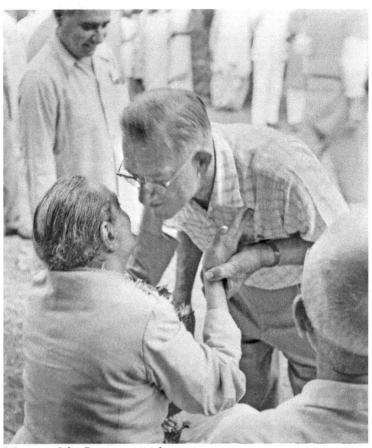

Westerner John Bass gets special attention

another quarter or half an hour, but Baba this time was adamant, although He was highly amused, and at six o'clock promptly He left, instructing us to return at once to Meherabad. Our last glimpse of Baba showed Him seated on top of His automobile, giving mass *darshan* to all those who had not been able to come before six. As we drove off, we heard shouts of *"Shri Sadguru Meher Baba Maharaj ki jai"* as Baba left for Pimpalgaon.

"I love them all, big and small"

Monday, September 27

Baba came in the morning, unexpectedly, when several of the group were not present. He said He did not want to come as He had to deal with other things; but the women had presents they wanted Him to give with His own hands, and to distribute photographs to which He had put His signature.

Mr. K. Hitaker, the Japanese, was called and told that from 12 mid-day until six o'clock tomorrow evening, he was to keep silence, to think of Baba and to read the messages.

Baba then explained what was to happen on the 29th and 30th. On the first day there were to be group talks and interviews, and we should come down to mix with the company and chat with them, but there was no need to stay there. We must, however, be there at 8:45 a.m. On the 30th, we were to be there at 8:45 a.m. and come away only when He said so.

He then distributed the presents and photographs, and said, "To all you meet and see, give My love — the only thing worth receiving." He said to Mr Hitaker, "You may become one of My chief workers in spreading My work in Japan and in other places, but you must first absorb Me and feel that you love Me. To tell others what we don't feel ourselves is hypocrisy. So feel, then speak with conviction. I will help you for I am in you. For the last seven nights I had no rest, but I am happy." He then embraced everyone and went away.

On June 6th, 1954, a circular had been sent out to those interested in Baba "as Baba," inviting them to the momentous meetings on the 29th and 30th. The first seven points are of interest:

Life Circular No. 18   Issued June 6, 1954

MEETING AT MEHERABAD
29th and 30th September 1954

(Exclusively for males above the age of 16)

1. Avatar Meher Baba desires to meet at Meherabad (Ahmednagar) on 29th and 30th Sept. 1954 his close disciples, devotees, associates and all those who love him, irrespective of whether at any time they saw him or did not see him.

2. Only those who are genuinely interested in Baba as "Baba" or in his work need take the trouble of going to him and avail themselves of the occasion of getting benefitted by his presence and getting a true understanding of his work.

3. In the meeting or meetings that will be held at Meherabad as above, Baba wants to make absolutely clear certain most important points, regarding his present

incarnation and his work in this life. Just as the Rajamundry meeting in Andhra State called for his work and workers and was the first and last of its kind, so also this Meherabad Meeting will be the first and last of its kind before he gives up his present physical body.

4. With the exception of Mass Darshan programme that will be held on 12th September 1954 at Ahmednagar proper, when he may give a message or messages, the above Meherabad meeting occasion will be the last for him to give message or messages.

5. Amongst the many phases of Baba's work, the one that signifies the act of giving messages will be discontinued from the beginning of October 1954 onwards. *They will veritably and literally be stopped.*

6. All those (males above the age of 16) who decide to go and attend the Meherabad meeting should fill in the Acceptance Form provided herewith, sign and send it, so as to reach Adi K. Irani not later than 1st August 1954.

7. All those who decide to attend the meeting should individually send as *dakshana* rupees twenty-two (Rs. 22/—) by a money order to Adi K. Irani to reach him not later than 1st August 1954.

NOTE: No one should bring with him female devotees. No one should bring with him male devotees below the age of 16. They will not be permitted to enter Meherabad.

Wednesday, September 29

The first of the two great final days: it had rained heavily from 4 a.m. on Tuesday until 4 a.m. this morning; most of the time a so-called "elephant rain," with a very high wind from the northwest, so that part of the wall surrounding Meherabad was broken down, and the water leaked in the refectory, dormitory and elsewhere.

A large *pandal* had been erected just off the roadway

near Meherabad, in which a thousand men could be seated. There were sleeping quarters, a place where they had their meals and a field kitchen. Owing to the heavy rain there was mud everywhere, and much discomfort must have been suffered by all the 948 devotees and workers for Baba who had come from all over India, at His invitation, to take part in the meetings.

The *pandal* was gaily decorated, with platform at the end for Baba. Baba arrived early. When all had gathered in the meeting *pandal*, Baba had this announced on the microphone:

"I called all you dear ones for the Meeting. What is meeting? Meeting means we meet. So before we begin anything, we meet in embrace for the last time. So meet Me with all your heart, but not so tightly so as to break My ribs!

"Last night, all the time I was thinking: Why the rains started, especially on the 28th when you all were to arrive here; because all these 28 days there was sunshine and all the programs went off very cheerfully. The darshan program of 12th September, the explanations to the Western group here, and another program at Sakori, where I went to lay My head at the shrine of My Master, and the program at 'Nagar on the 26th at Sarosh Motor Works, went off cheerfully.

"Then for the first time I asked Myself, whether I was the Avatar; and the clear and definite answer was, 'Yes, I am the Ancient One, the Highest of the High,' Then I asked Avatar Meher Baba, 'why this rain — this inconvenience to the lovers who have come all the way to meet You!' Avatar Meher Baba replied, 'Those who really love You would come with their heads on their palms, and this inconvenience would be a happiness to them.'

"In all parts of India, every year thousands of pilgrims go to pay their homage to the holy places and the tombs of the Saints and Masters, undergoing all kinds of hardships on the way — sometimes journeying long distances on foot, and many die on the way from illness, exposure and contamination of disease, none of which deter them from their objective. How much more hardship and inconvenience you should be prepared to undergo therefore, when you come to the living Master! For, instead of the ordinary pilgrimage to tombs and holy relics of the past, you are gathered today at the shrine of the living Avatar, Meher Baba.

"Now after embracing you all, one after the other, for the last time, be brave and confess your weaknesses, because very soon I am going to destroy all the bindings of the religious ceremonies."

Everybody joins in a queue to pass Baba for this last embrace.

"As I am going to drop My body soon, this is your last opportunity to embrace Me. By God's Will may you all be worthy of My Love, and not sell Me."

While the queue was passing, one of the men, before he reached Baba, started sobbing bitterly. Baba was in great good humor, and was joking with many of those who came to Him, and patted many on the shoulder.

Disciples from Andhra introduced themselves and told how Jean's book *Avatar* drew them to Baba, and how grateful they were for it, as well as for this meeting and being here with us. Pleader came to greet us. Dastur was seated on the platform, repeating Baba's Name. Nawal Talati's son, Kurshed, came to greet us.

At 9:30 a.m. the prayers were said. They were the same prayers — Zoroastrian, Moslem, Christian, and "The Praise of the Ten Incarnations," all which had been uttered on Friday the 17th, with the addition of a prayer to Guru Nanak, spoken by Dr. Daulat Singh in Sikh language. Again, Baba took active part in the prayers. At one time during the prayers, there was an interruption by someone acclaiming Baba, which was instantly checked by Baba.

After the prayers, Baba asked if anyone felt tired, as He would give an interval before the Confession; adding,

"Baba never feels tired; if you are not tired, we will go on." All cried that they were not tired. Baba then said "Pay proper attention and make this Confession for yourselves and for all the world with all your hearts. God is deaf to the language of the mind, and keen to hear only the language of the heart. If you put your heart into My Confession, God will definitely make you love Him." This was translated into Hindi, Marathi, Gujarati, and Telegu, as were all the other statements made during the meeting.

Baba said: "What is known as virtue and sin are nothing but strength and weakness."

Then followed the Confession as made on Friday the 17th of September with the addition of a Confession to Guru Nanak by Dr. Daulat Singh in Sikh language.

Baba then said: "You are now free to call out 'jai!' or anything you like," and He called for Francis Brabazon to come to the microphone and to cry "*Avatar Meher Baba ki jai!*" which was repeated loudly by all the company. Baba then said that all were free to disperse and that from 2 o'clock onwards He would call groups and give talks to them, and also give a few private talks. He told the Westerners to go up the hill and stay there. He also said, "Whether it rains or not, be here tomorrow morning at 9 o'clock and in the afternoon at 3:30 p.m., when I will say precisely for the last time what I have to say."

Thursday, September 30

The day was cool and cloudy, with a little sun, but no rain. Instructions had been given previously that none of the devotees was to go up the hill. The crowd of men, over 900, was waiting for Baba at the railroad tracks, and when Baba appeared at 9 a.m., they made a path for Him to pass through. He then led the whole company up the hill. When they arrived outside the ashram they all rested, and Baba sat under a tree near the gate, looking down the hill. He allowed pictures to be taken of Himself and the crowd,

Outside the ashram, Meherabad hill, on day of Meher Baba's Final Declaration.

then led the way to the tomb, after explaining through Eruch, Kaka, and two other men in four different languages, that He wanted the assembled men to see the tomb, His last resting-place. Baba then got up and went to the tomb. All sat outside and Baba repeated what He had already said to us about the tomb. Also He told about the boy who drank half the coffee that was sent to Him during seclusion, and said, "For one complete year I took the *prasad* of that boy." The boy's name was Laher.

He explained that the boarded-up window on the south side was formerly open, and during the period He was there, He sometimes put His legs outside, and the boys of the Prem Ashram used to gather to take *darshan*. That was where the boy Chota Baba got his great spiritual experience; he was unconscious of the gross world for three days. "I had Pleader locked up in a small room here for two and a half years when he had milk only, and was given the order to keep silence and not to write. May God one day make him realize that Baba is the only Reality, the Highest of the High. When Pleader was locked up, a cobra came and hung over his head, but he did not move or call because of Baba's order. The cobra was there for three days and used to drink his milk. Then the one who brought the milk saw the cobra, informed the Mandali, one of whom came and killed the cobra. My Mandali who have been staying with Me for years would lay down their lives at My bidding."

Baba said there was no time to visit the place where He sat for months in complete seclusion, only communicating with the Mandali through a slit in the wall, but He pointed out where it was. The company then visited the tomb one by one. He then called the Western group to have a photograph taken, inquired from each about his health, and told them to go to the *pandal* to get good seats.

All then returned to the *pandal*, and at 9:30 a.m. Baba entered the tent, mounted the platform and took His seat on the couch. Before He entered, the company was instructed not to rise on His entrance. He sat on the couch and looked at the company.

He said: "Before I give My Final Declaration, I want to say a few words regarding other matters. After the meeting, I shall leave promptly. All who want to get the full benefit of this meeting, and return home with the atmosphere of this place, I wish them to go directly after the meeting to their destination. If Baba-lovers from the North or the South want to stay at Bombay or other places, it would mean that they had not come to Baba only, but to talk or to play or to attend to their own affairs, so I want all to return to their destinations at once. One devotee from Jubbulpore has asked if he might go to Panchgani and has been told that he must return home, and afterwards go to Panchgani if he wants to."

Baba said: "Before the Declaration, I will say a few words about My Masters. Today, during both sessions, I shall be precise in what I want to convey to you." He then asked for the men from Sakori, five of whom came on to the platform and sat down. He said: "What I am, what I was, and what I will be as the Ancient One is always due to the five Perfect Masters of the Age. Sai Baba, Upasni Maharaj, Babajan, Tajuddin Baba and Narayan Maharaj — these are the five Perfect Masters of this Age for Me."

He interrupted one of the interpreters to say to him that he appeared excited and confused, "because you think I am going to drop this body," continued Baba; "but I am not going to drop the body today!" Baba then went on. "Only Maharaj and Babajan directly played the main roles. Babajan, in less than a millionth of a second, made Me realize that I am God; and in the period of seven years, Upasni Maharaj gave me the Divine Knowledge that I am the Avatar. Before Maharaj dropped His body, We physically met in a secluded place." At this point Baba again called the translator to account and asked him to repeat only the words he spelt out on the board and not to interpret them. He went on: "And before I drop My body, I had to meet Him, so I went to Sakori and bowed down to His shrine and told Him, 'You know I am the Ancient One.' "

Baba again interrupted the translator and replaced him with another. He went on: "Maharaj was Perfection personified. At the head of the Sakori Ashram is Godavri Mai, whom I call 'Yashoda.'* She is a unique female personality and loves Me beyond words, and to Me she is the dearest of the dear. Today you will be shown the pictures of My visit to Sakori so that you may feel you too were there."

Baba then introduced the Sakori men. He first asked Yeshwantrao to rise, and said: "He is the link between Maharaj and Merwan." Mr. Wagh then stood up and Baba said: "This is Mr. Wagh, who has for years faithfully and

*Mother of Krishna.

honestly carried out the office work and the arrangements at Sakori Ashram; he can be called one of the few main pillars of Sakori." Mr. Vasant Deshmukh stood up and Baba said: "Here is Sakori's high priest; even his priesthood will not save Me from the violent death." Mr. Purandhare stood up and Baba said: "One of the most honest, faithful workers at Sakori." Then Dr. Bharucha stood up and Baba said: "This old Hindu father loves God wholeheartedly and longs for God, at Sakori, near the feet of Maharaj." The Sakori men then left the platform.

Baba said: "Now please pay attention, be wide awake, not drowsy. Since I stopped speaking, and also stopped writing, except for My signature, when essential, I carried on with this alphabet board all these years of My Silence. From the 7th of October, 1954, I will give up this board too, and I won't make signs with My fingers, like Gustadji, to convey thoughts. From the 7th of October, I shall not be speaking, writing, or using the board, or making signs with My fingers. I shall be as if withdrawing within Myself. This is because now at last the so-long-promised and repeatedly promised time of breaking My Silence is very near. From the 7th October, 1954, I shall completely retire from My present activities. There will be no mass *darshan*, no programs, no meetings, no messages, nor correspondence. Take this seriously and do not write to Me from the 7th October, as I shall pay no attention to letters. I shall go with Gadejai Maharaj when he takes Me to Pandharpur, if he has the fortune to do this, as I shall drop this body soon. The Mandali have asked me today to say in a few words exactly and precisely what will happen to Me. So I tell you, note it down:

"In October at Satara, I shall be appearing to lead a retired, normal life, eating, taking walks, and so on; but there will be no use of the board and other things from 7th October, as I have told you. By the end of April, 1955, I shall definitely drop this body. During the six months, November, December, January, February, March and

April, three phases of the Avatar-life will manifest themselves. First, a very strange and serious disease will attack this body, which will be the cause of My humiliation that I have been speaking about. Secondly, the humiliation will end in the sudden breaking of My Silence, and My uttering that Word which only God can utter. Thirdly, Glorification will replace humiliation. All the pent-up Infinity in Me will splash and spread over the Universe."

Baba then called for Donkin and said to him that what followed was important, that he must grasp it and convey it over the microphone. Donkin then spoke the following: "Baba wants to use a simile about the atom bomb. Just as an atom bomb, which in itself is so small, when exploded, causes tremendous havoc, so, when He breaks His Silence, the universal spiritual upheaval that will take place will be something that no one can describe. It will happen in a second, at a time when nobody expects it. Just as when an earthquake takes place suddenly, when no one is ready, and no one can do anything, but everyone in the affected area feels it, so the breaking of My Silence will create a spiritual upheaval and everyone will feel it in his heart.

"And, unbelievable as it may seem, My universal Glorification will not be manifested very near My physical Presence, wherever I may then be. At the time of My Glorification, all will feel it throughout the world, but those who are around Me will not be affected. They who will be there will not be merely disinterested in Baba, they will actually be hostile. For example, I may then be in Poona, with no one from the Mandali near Me, but thirty or forty of the hostile group may be there, and they will not feel this Glorification and upheaval. All the rest of the world will feel it. No one of My Mandali or lovers will be near Me when I am beaten and finally stabbed.

"Yet I never die. I am always the Ancient One. You should all remember that God alone is real and all else is illusion.

"Your attending this meeting and hearing in precise

and definite terms about these happenings will be worth it if all of you, or if some of you, or at least a few of you, spread the message of My love to others."

The above was heard in deep silence. Baba then said that from 3 o'clock, His Final Declaration would be read in all the four languages, and that from 5 o'clock, all would be free to depart and that all must depart by tomorrow noon. After lunch, all would have the opportunity to look at the Sakori pictures. They were asked not to try to embrace Baba as He left, or to garland Him, or to ask Him for anything. He asked the Western group to go up the hill and to come down again at 3 p.m.

At 2:40 p.m. when everyone had assembled, Baba was outside the *pandal* and entered at 2:50 p.m., taking His seat. The company was told not to rise. He then asked for five young men and said to them: "You asked for this, so I give you ten minutes." They then sang a hymn to Baba. Baba expressed great appreciation in gestures, and sent them back to their seats.

At 3 o'clock precisely, Eruch read Baba's Final Declaration (see page 114). The Declaration and the four translations were received in complete silence. There was not a single movement from any of the company. During the reading of the first translation, one of the Mandali, sitting in the first row, appeared to be asleep. Baba noticed him and sent Eruch to him to waken him and bring him on to the platform where Baba spoke to him and made him stand until all the translations were finished. Baba had Padri pat His back four times while the second version was read. Once He gesticulated for a glass of water which was brought to Him. He listened attentively to a very eloquent and dramatic reading. During the third reading, Baba was quieter, and expressed approval to Eruch, while the reading continued. Deshmukh read the fourth version, and Baba asked Eruch if everyone could hear clearly. Baba sat on the edge of the couch, then moved on to the steps. Then Baba distributed *prasad;* the assembly broke up, and

Baba went away.

It should be added that the arrangements for the meetings, all of which had to be improvised, were most efficiently carried through by Pendu and Padri. There was hot water for everyone, and good food was provided. An emergency electric light supply was fitted throughout the *pandal* and the other buildings, operated from the Meherabad flour mill for the villagers. The comfort of everybody was attended to, and the Mandali worked extremely hard for days to make sure that everything went off without a hitch. Transport facilities were provided to and from the Ahmednagar station to Meherabad, supervised by Vishnu and Dattu, and train accommodation was looked after by Chinchawade.

Thus was brought to a close the most remarkable experience of our lives. The Western group found the Indian devotees most friendly and had many good talks with them. A large proportion of the devotees were young men, but there were young and old, and men of every type, a large assembly of deeply interested men. The quietness and orderly behavior of everyone throughout the two days was impressive; and simplicity, sincerity, absence of display and intense seriousness were notable characteristics. That Baba was in control throughout was certain, but so lightly and unobtrusively that it was hardly to be noticed.

The Western group left Meherabad on the hill in the evening from Ahmednagar for Bombay, where they dispersed to their homes during the following few days.

———————●———————

Meher Baba's Final Declaration
At His Last Meeting
At Meherabad
On September 30th, 1954

"I am very happy to have you all here.

"I know that very many of you have come to Meherabad under greatly difficult circumstances. Some of you have covered thousands of miles, and even crossed continents to be at Meherabad today. It is your deep love for Me that has braved all obstacles and prompted you to sacrifice your comforts and convenience to honor My Call and to be near Me today.

"I am deeply touched by your devotion and I am proud of the hearts that contain such love and loyalty.

"There are many more devoted hearts like yours yearning to be present here, but these are not to be seen in your midst today. I know that in spite of their intense desire to be near Me, they could not possibly come, for one reason or another. Therefore they depend upon you to convey to them in detail all that you see and hear during this two days of unique opportunity that has fallen to your lot. I trust you will not fail them.

"Although you are present here with all love and faith in Me and though you feel blessed to have My personal contact, yet I know that you will not realize today, as you ought to, the true significance of My Call and your presence here at this juncture. Time alone will make most of you realize, not many months from now, the significant importance of this assembly.

"The time is fast approaching when all that I have repeatedly stressed, from time to time, will definitely come to pass. Most of you will witness those events, and will recall very vividly all that transpires during these two days of your stay at Meherabad.

"I have come not to establish anything new — I have come to put life into the old. I have not come to establish retreats or ashrams. I create them for the purpose of My universal work, only to repeatedly dissolve them once that purpose has been served.

"The universe is My ashram, and every heart is My house; but I manifest only in those hearts in which all, other than Me, ceases to live.

"When My Universal Religion of Love is on the verge of fading into insignificance, I come to breathe life into it and to do away with the farce of dogmas that defile it in the name of religions and stifle it with ceremonies and rituals.

"The present universal confusion and unrest has filled the heart of man with greater lust for power and a greed for wealth and face, bringing in its wake untold misery, hatred, jealousy, frustration and fear. Suffering in the world is at its height, in spite of all the striving to spread peace and prosperity, to bring about a lasting happiness.

"For man to have a glimpse of lasting happiness he has first to realize that God, being in all, knows all; that God alone acts and reacts through all; that God, in the guise of countless animate and inanimate entities, experiences the innumerably varied phenomena of suffering and happiness, and that God Himself undergoes all these illusory happenings. Thus, it is God Who has brought suffering in human experience to its height, and God alone Who will efface this illusory suffering and bring the illusory happiness to its height.

"Whether it manifests as Creation or disappears into the Oneness of Reality, whether it is experienced as existing and real, or is perceived to be false or non-existent, illusion throughout is illusion. There is no end to it, just as there is no end to imagination.

"There are two aspects experienced in illusion — manyness and oneness. While manyness multiplies manyness, oneness goes on magnifying itself. Manyness is the 'religion' of illusion on which illusion thrives.

"In the illusory beginning of Time, there was no such state of mess in illusion as there is today. When the evolution of consciousness began, there was oneness, in spite of the diversity in illusion. With the growth of consciousness, manyness also went on increasing, until now it is about to overlap the limit. Like the wave that reaches its crest, this height of manyness will dissolve itself and bring about the beginning of oneness in illusion. Suffering at its height will cause destruction of this climax of manyness in illusion.

"The time has come for the pre-ordained destruction of multiple separateness which keeps man from experiencing the feeling of unity and brotherhood. This destruction which will take place very soon, will cause three-fourths of the world to be destroyed. The remaining one-fourth will be brought together to live a life of concord and mutual understanding, thus establishing a feeling of oneness in all fellow beings, leading them towards lasting happiness.

"Before I break My silence or immediately after it, three-fourths of the world will be destroyed. I shall speak soon to fulfil all that is shortly to come to pass.

"To affirm religious faiths, to establish societies, or to hold conferences will never bring about the feeling of unity and oneness in the life of mankind, now completely absorbed in the manyness of illusion. Unity in the midst of diversity can be made to be felt only by touching the very core of the heart. That is the work for which I have come.

"I have come to sow the seed of love in your hearts so that, in spite of all superficial diversity which your life in illusion must experience and endure, the feeling of oneness, through love, is brought about amongst all the nations, creeds, sects and castes of the world.

"In order to bring this about, I am preparing to break My Silence. When I break My Silence it will not be to fill your ears with spiritual lectures. I shall speak only One

Word, and this Word will penetrate the hearts of all men and make even the sinner feel that he is meant to be a saint, while the saint will know that God is in the sinner as much as He is in himself.

"When I speak that Word, I shall lay the foundation for that which is to take place during the next seven hundred years. When I come again after seven hundred years, the evolution of consciousness will have reached such an apex that materialistic tendencies will be automatically transmuted into spiritual longing, and the feeling of equality in universal brotherhood will prevail. This means that opulence and poverty, literacy and illiteracy, jealousy and hatred, which are in evidence today in their full measure, will then be dissolved through the feeling of the oneness of all men. Prosperity and happiness will then be at their zenith.

"This does not mean that oneness in illusion shall remain so eternally. That is because all this that is, is illusion, and the consciousness of oneness as well as of manyness in illusion is part of the process of evolution. The time is bound to recur when there will be again the same beginning, growth and culmination of the heights of manyness and oneness in illusion.

"My next advent, after I drop this body, will be after seven hundred years, and that will mark the end and the beginning of a Cycle of Cycles. All cycles of time in illusion end and begin after 700 to 1,400 years, and there have been and will be millions and billions of such cycles in a Cycle of Cycles; thus, there is no end to illusion, which always remains illusion.

"Age after age I come amidst mankind to maintain My own Creation of Illusion, thereby also awakening humanity to become aware of it. The framework of illusion is always one and the same, but the designs in illusion are innumerable and everchanging. My advent is not to destroy illusion because illusion, as it is, is absolutely nothing. I come to make you become aware of the nothingness of illusion. Through *you* I automatically maintain illusion, which is nothing but the shadow of My Infinite Self, and through *Me* you automatically discard illusion when you are made aware of its falseness.

"My manifestation as the Avatar of the time will be of short duration. This short period will, in quick succession, cover My humiliation, the breaking of My silence, My glorification and My violent physical end. Everlastingly with all the Divine Bliss within Me, I eternally suffer for one and all — thus I am crucified eternally and continually for all.

"During this short period, My Word of Words will touch the hearts of all mankind, and spontaneously this Divine touch will instil in man the feeling of the oneness of all fellow beings. Gradually, in the course of the next seven hundred years, this feeling will supersede the tendency of separateness and rule over the hearts of all, driving away hatred, jealousy and greed that breed suffering, and happiness will reign."

Explanatory Notes on the Final Declaration By Meher Baba

Given November 13, 1954, at Satara, India

The following explanatory notes given by Baba to His Mandali in India, conveyed through gestures, are to clarify certain points of His Final Declaration of September 30th, 1954. Baba states that this explanation will greatly ease the tension of His devotees who feel much worried or confused over His words in the Final Declaration.

Meher Baba had mentioned during the Meherabad meeting His intended visit to Pandharpur, which would be His very last public appearance. Thus, although Baba has stopped using His alphabet board and has stopped giving darshan, He kept His promise to the saint Gadejai Maharaj and visited Pandharpur on November 6th, where tens of thousands of people were blessed by Baba's Presence.

The day following His visit to Pandharpur, Baba gave to His Mandali, through the use of gestures, the following explanation:

"It is really very difficult for any one to believe and understand what I say, because none can grasp the meaning underlying My words. It is natural even for My intimate Mandali not to understand My Final Declaration; but I want you to take everything that I said in Meherabad during the Meetings very seriously because all that I said was the truth, they were words of God, and all the things said must come to pass exactly in the manner described by Me.

"From the day I declared in Meherabad that there will be the destruction of three-fourths of the world, that a strange disease will attack My body, that I will suffer humiliation, that I will break My Silence, and speak One Word, the Word of Words, that there will be My Glorification, and that finally I will drop My body when I shall be stabbed in the back, My lovers and others have been unnecessarily confused, and they all have been trying to interpret My words in different ways.

"Everyone is free to interpret My words in any way they think and feel. But one thing I tell you, that whenever I say a thing I naturally use My own 'language,' and whatsoever is said by Me is Truth. But, My 'language' is such that none can understand or grasp the underlying meaning of what I say; therefore, when I want to say a thing I have simultaneously to make use of your language also, knowing well that you would understand nothing whatsoever if I were to make use of My 'language' alone.

"In order to help you to understand My Final Declaration, and to put an end to your confusion and worry, I want all of you to know that when you saw Me dictate on My alphabet board during the Meetings at Meherabad, and heard about:

1) A strange disease attacking My body: it was said in your language.

2) The humiliation that I will suffer: it was said in your language.

3) The breaking of My Silence and My uttering the One Word of words: it was said in My own 'language' and simultaneously in yours, because when I utter that Word, it will be an audible word to you.

4) My Glorification: it was said simultaneously in My 'language' and in yours.

5) The destruction of three-fourths of the world: it was said in My own 'language' alone.

6) The stab in My back: it was said in My own 'language' alone.

7) The dropping of My body: it was said in My own 'language' and simultaneously in yours.

"Consequently, whatever is said by Me in *your* language, you are able to understand and know what is said; but, that which is said in *My own 'language'* is impossible for you to understand, however much you may all try to interpret and grasp the underlying meaning behind My words. Only the fulfillment of events can unfold to you, in due course, the meaning of what is said in My own 'language.'

"I therefore want you all not to worry unnecessarily or be confused. Just believe that whatever I say is Truth; and that all that I said in My Final Declaration will come to pass precisely as I have dictated, by the end of April, 1955. And, the beginning of all that is to happen within the period of these six months will be effected by Me from the 1st of December, 1954."

Facets of the Diamond

By Baba's Western Devotees

Baba is Truth, Baba is Love, He is Divinity in action, in the human form. He is beyond the power of any one individual mind or heart to grasp. Like a huge diamond blazing in the sun, He can only be seen from one facet at a time. During the "Three Incredible Weeks," from September 11th to September 30th, 1954, when His men devotees were with Him in India, each saw Him from his own viewpoint. Here are a few "facets" of their great experience, which they kindly share with us.

From Fred Marks:

August, 1954, on board the S.S. Corfu

This voyage from London to India at Baba's invitation is my first visit to India. On leaving Southampton, I was pleasantly surprised when returning to my cabin to see a display of photographs of Baba and to have Mr. Dana Field from New York, who is also on his way to visit Baba, share the cabin with me.

During this brief interval, before arriving at Bombay, there are on this boat groups of nearly all the principle Western and Eastern religions which hope to take up various activities in different parts of the world.

With infectious good humor, Dana says one has been reading the Bible to him and trying to "convert him." Such is the sincerity shown by some who in spiritual awakening turn feelingly towards others.

Some have received Baba's Universal Message and a few are showing still a deeper interest.

There is a general expectancy of a great happening.

The end of the Age brings again the urge and longing for the One who will bring Redemption and save humanity from the abyss into which it has fallen.

To find this One is to knowingly feel that there is nothing more to be desired.

It is the end of the quest.

His name today is MEHER BABA.

He offers Himself to us.

Baba is Light. He is the dynamo from which all spiritual activity proceeds.

He is human and Divine, His the Divine Will speeding through the channel of our being, Divine Love and Order.

I go to be accepted by Him.

From Lud Dimpfl :

In various conversations with persons who had stayed

with Baba for different lengths of time, more than a few mentioned the atmosphere of love which prevailed. Prior to my stay at Meherabad last September, I had no concept of how such an environment could differ from everyday situations.

The first two days at Meherabad, I was on my "best behavior." It seemed to me that the other "Westerners" were also. When Baba arrived to see our group for the first time on September 14, we gathered around Him and introduced ourselves. After this, Baba spelled out on the board, "I want you all to be completely natural with each other; not strained." Never have I desired more to do something and felt so unable. How does one act naturally? Baba did not dwell on the subject, but left it as soon as He had brought it up.

It was only an hour or so later that several of the Mandali approached me separately. They each asked whether there was anything about the accommodations, the service, the food — anything — that I didn't like. If so, please let them know. They would do their best to correct it. It seemed to me that Baba must have said to them, "See how unhappy and strained these people are. You must do more for them." And yet our accommodations and their considerations were as perfect as they could possibly be. This had the effect of intensifying my desire to be natural as Baba wished.

During the weeks that followed, the feeling of distance and need for correctness did start to dissolve. It was a dissolving rather than anything forced. Baba does not move a person by *repelling* him from avenues which he should not follow. Baba is simply *attractive.*

When an incident such as the foregoing strikes me as much as it did, I am predisposed to assume that others see these events in the identical light. This is always a dangerous generalization, but is more so around Baba. Incident after incident occurs with its peculiarly lingering forcefulness. Any one of them could be dismissed as coincidence, but not all. The best illustration of this is the story which Ramjoo told a group of four or five of us one morning.

Ramjoo Abdullah has been with Baba since 1921. This is the story of how he came to be associated with Him. In the Ahmednagar district in the early twenties there were many discussion circles — some Parsee, some Mohammedan, some Hindu. Ramjoo was a member of a Mohammedan circle led by Dr. Ghani. Baba, who was still widely addressed as Merwan in those days, used to visit many of these circles, among them the circle of which Ramjoo was a member. He would sort of "look over" the members of these circles for potential disciples. Many members of these circles had already become adherents of Baba's. Members of Ramjoo's circle had become Baba devotees and urged Ramjoo to follow Baba also, but Ramjoo did not feel so motivated and remained aloof.

Ramjoo lived in Bombay. In November, 1921, Baba's group came down from Poona for a boat outing to one of the islands near Bombay. Some of Ramjoo's friends in the group invited him along. Ramjoo accepted indifferently, and went because he had nothing else to do.

Once aboard ship, Ramjoo noticed that this was no ordinary discussion group. The members acted toward Baba not as equals, but as disciples. Baba was then not yet observing silence, and discoursed freely to the group. Suddenly He said, "Look at Bombay. Doesn't Bombay look beautiful?" All granted that Bombay looked beautiful receding in the distance. "No," said Baba, "that's not what I mean. A few moments ago we were in Bombay. Then we had to look up at the buildings, and had to turn our heads around to see them all. They seemed so much bigger than we. Now all of Bombay can be framed in our fingers." All agreed that this was an interesting and remarkable point. "No," said Baba, "you still don't understand. Is it Bombay which is small, or is it we who are small?"

That ended the discussion and Baba went on to other subjects. This, however, stuck in Ramjoo's mind and bothered him. Try as he would, he could not get it out. So he started to steal glances at Baba to see whether He was watching him, but Baba never took notice of him and went unconcernedly on as ever discoursing to the group. Ramjoo wondered about Him, and the point continued to occupy his mind — Is Bombay small, or are we small?

The ship was too large to land at the island, and the passengers were rowed ashore in small boats. By coincidence, Baba and Ramjoo were in one boat-load together. But even with this close contact, Baba seemed unaware of and unconcerned with Ramjoo.

Mohammedans pray five times daily. Although this custom is observed by the older generation, the younger ones in that part of India seldom do, although Ramjoo, who was then 22, did faithfully say his five prayers a day. So about 1:30 p.m. he left the group, found a secluded alcove on the beach, and said his prayers. When he rejoined the party, Baba was scolding them. He said, "Here I come on a picnic with you and what do you do? Some go off fishing, some to say their prayers, some... "

"Well," thought Ramjoo, "He's guessing. Possibly others say their prayers regularly also. I'll just find out." So Ramjoo contacted each member of the group individually, and said, "Well, (so and so), I see you left Merwan's company to say your prayers." The invariable answer was, "I don't know about the others, but I wasn't saying prayers." So Ramjoo was the only one who had said prayers. Still Ramjoo thought Baba was guessing. After all, equipment is required for fishing — nets, hooks, line, bait — and no one had fishing equipment along. So Ramjoo approached one of the group and said "What does Merwan mean, we left Him to go fishing? Everyone knows you need equipment to fish." "Well," said the other, "I don't know about you, but I was fishing. I dug a trench in the beach with my hands, waited for the fish to swim into it, then blocked off the opening." This, then, had not been mere guessing.

Now Ramjoo had a collection of shells and pretty colored stones. While walking along the beach he had found many for his collection. His pockets were filled. He had made a haul. On the ship on the way back Baba again discoursed to the group. He said that it was the nature of men to collect things. Some collect possessions, some money, some objects of art. Men collect all kinds of things. "It would not surprise Me," He said, "if someone even collected those little shells and pebbles off beaches." Everyone guffawed loudly at this last statement. Secretly and unostentatiously, Ramjoo emptied his pockets over the side, handful by handful.

When they got back to Bombay, Baba sat in a circle with His group, and gave them all an opportunity to ask Him questions. The first one designated to ask a question sat next to Ramjoo and the questioning went around the circle away from him so that he would be the last. Ramjoo noticed that the questions were all of a personal nature dealing with individuals' problems. Ramjoo did not want to speak to Baba in front of this group. He wanted to speak to Him privately. So Ramjoo was dreading his turn. Baba however stopped the questions just short of Ramjoo. "This is just fine," thought Ramjoo. But one of the group addressed Baba, calling attention to the fact that Ramjoo hadn't had his turn. Ramjoo thought, "Here everything was working out so well and this fellow has to spoil it." But Baba simply said, "I intend to speak to Ramjoo later."

Baba called Ramjoo into His compartment on the train for Poona. He addressed Ramjoo in an authoritative tone. "I happen to be in a position where I can give you anything you want," He said, "wealth, rich possessions, fame, everything. I therefore give you the choice of two alternatives. Either you ask of Me anything you want and I will give it to you, or you agree to do anything I tell you to do from now on." Ramjoo was tongue-tied and taken

aback. Baba continued, "I advise you to ask something —
anything — so this matter can now be finished and I can
wash My hands of it, and you also. I will stick to my bargain
and give you anything you wish. But you must choose
between this or obeying My orders from now on." Ramjoo
was silent. "Well," said Baba, "you don't have to decide
now. But think about it and give me your answer." About
half an hour later Baba said, "Are you still thinking?" "No,"
said Ramjoo. "Why not, when I have told you to?" asked
Baba. "Because I have made up my mind," said Ramjoo, "I
have decided to obey Your orders."

Baba then instructed Ramjoo to repeat any name of
God for one hour each day. This Ramjoo did, and when
Baba asked him the next day whether he had done so,
(Ramjoo expected He would ask), Ramjoo said that he had.
But Ramjoo did not expect the next question. "Which name
of God did you use?" Baba asked. Ramjoo answered, "I
used Your name, Baba."

From Dana Field:

Meherabad, September 18, 1954

My very dear ————:

Sahebji from Meherabad Hill! I hope you are not fooled
into thinking I know Marathi. The great drama that is
unfolding before us daily drives all other thoughts from
the mind. Besides, Baba has given us the assignment of
one-half hour daily silence, and He is with us for a few
hours. We have been taken to a number of historic places,
and for tea to the Bank.

Baba seems to be aging daily. He says He is crucified,
every moment, which He gladly is, so that one should love
our God. He said His body will be destroyed, perhaps in
December, and none of the Mandali will be near Him. It
seems to me that someone should stay with Him, of the
Western disciples.... Meanwhile, He is lavishing love and
plenty on all of us and I am getting more than the lion's

share. I may have pleased Him by translating a song by Yma Sumac, played on the phonograph this a.m. He said He wished someone would love Him that way: — "I love only Thee; I worship only Thee; to Thee alone I surrender the key to my treasure." Baba enjoyed Yma Sumac, — "As long as she comes down from the highest to the lowest notes, I feel happy because it reminds me of what I am doing." Just previously He had asked, "Can any one imagine how I can be here and everywhere at the same time?"

As we were listening with Baba to the records, a Japanese young man arrived to see Baba. He had a very reverent attitude, and was embraced by Baba who said, "He loves the Truth." He had come all the way from Japan to see Baba, about whom a Theosophy leader had informed him. He wants Baba to come to Japan. Baba promised to do so, after 700 years. He is related to the Ambassador of Japan to India, and will be back for the *darshan*, after which Baba will give him a glimpse of Himself if he meditates for one week here. He was given a royal meal. He could not have arrived more dramatically. Baba told him he was very fortunate, because He does not permit people on the hill. I wasn't so fortunate — I forgot my kleenex and the tears caused my nose to run!

Tomorrow, Indian songs will be played; and Baba will explain a few mysteries. I'll give you the titles of those played.... Baba asked us to keep our consciousness here and "try to absorb as much of Baba as you can." I just took a walk over to the flowers, which is my way of refreshing myself, and I felt as if I could fly away; the combination of spiritual consciousness and the beauties of nature, wind, and sky is overwhelming.

I must ask you to forgive my slighting news about individuals here. I shouldn't, and in fact I was personally affected by the others, except for Marks and Backett, even whose surface is saintly. Too much human nature for me, as I am sensitive and critical in the first place, and the contrast with Baba was so great. But I assure you we have been welded into a unit by Baba, and there is only love and peace. Dr. Donkin is close to Baba, although very different. He is our medic. Very handsome and healthy, but also apparently gentle. Francis Brabazon is Baba's comedian. His surface is hard but his heart's right.... Right now he is scolding our dog who got himself chewed up when he attacked his own father (mistaken identity, no doubt)! Baba put Francis in charge of the two Australian boys, whom He told to stay in His tomb at 12 midnight for half an hour. They are to sit on the edge of the pit, and if they fall and break a leg, Baba will hold him responsible! They are to keep eyes open and not blink. I suggested they take a nap this afternoon.

We just had tea. I am so full of the good food that Mrs. Irani feeds us that I am considering putting a sign on myself, "no more room." Yet, Baba had mentioned yesterday that we don't seem to have enough, as far as He could see! So, we're getting more than ever. Baba gave us prasad of "Sitafal" fruit, laying His hands on us from the back as we sat at table. His humility is boundless. Today He sat on the floor, covered with a tablecloth, while we ate. The Sufi men are terrifically impressed and in tears half the time. Baba "spoke" in Arabic or Persian to Joseph Harb — it meant "Everlasting Breath." Yesterday we were permitted the privilege of being at Baba's prayers, in several languages. He prayed in front of His own picture, giant size. "Today God has joined you in praying to God," He remarked to us when we were in the Hall today. It was a very impressive ceremony, without priests or temples, etc. When Baba does anything, it takes on life and meaning; the old familiar songs we heard had a new flavor.

During the meeting this a.m. Baba, as usual, was doing His Universal Work. He says that being here and there at the same time is called *Sahaj Samadhi*. He distinguished for us between a trance state which is momentary ecstasy but does not result in a changed individual; several states of *Samadhi,* after which comes distress as a result of a sort of (spiritual) drunkenness; and *Nirvikalpa Samadhi (Fana* in Sufism) or real Union with God. But many do not regain worldly consciousness. *Sahaj* (effortless, spontaneous) or *Nirvikalpa Samadhi* operates on every plane. He promised to explain how He does it.

Mr. Purdom told me not to ask Baba to stay with Him, and told me a story to illustrate. A disciple of Baba said his greatest desire was to visit the Taj Mahal Hotel in Bombay. He was dressed up and taken there but he kept slipping and falling at the entrance, so they threw him out for a drunk. Baba's will be done! He knows what He wants!

We were given a silence discipline half-hour daily. Today I had a hard time of it because of fever. Also I sat on the ground and this is not a comfortable position. We have to try to picture Baba, a wonderful spiritual exercise.

I just had a talk with Malcolm, Baba is keeping him busy editing notes. I was reminded of several points in my conversation with Baba which had slipped my mind: to use my mind but to be its master; to enjoy Maya, but overcome a negative emotion with an opposite, stronger one, and thus avoid *sanskaras;* let the bad thought go, without suppressing it, and act on the good one; the ego is necessary in our development but must be transcended. (Baba had spoken of the natural, false and divine ego). I shall make it a point to seek out Malcolm as I was helped through our conversation.

In connection with my doubts, Baba said, "Moses and Peter doubted and denied Me, and served Me imperfectly and you will too..." When I asked about my former guru, referring to him as a 'great soul,' (Mahatma) — Baba said, "Don't call people great souls. Greatness of soul is on the plane of Perfection. Don't criticise him. Forget him. He is working within illusion..."

A point of interest about India: they don't seem to have a Sunday. *Guruvar* is on Thursday (Master's Day), Moslems have their Friday. A case of the lost weekend.

Had dinner. It's a beautiful night, as only India or other tropical highlands can have. The air is soft. Again I wonder at our being here, in the hands and heart of the Avatar. What is the destiny, what are the root causes that have brought us to Him? In any case, I would not exchange my present situation for the world's kingdoms. The Kingdom of God is real, rich, and it is within us. The outer is our own projection, Baba tells us. We are here to gain a pure heart, to learn to truly love, and thus see God. Baba's role among us is so incredible, being on all planes simultaneously, that it is inconceivable to us. It is good to wonder at the truly wonderful, rather than at curiosities. I wish I could retain all that He is giving us but it's impossible; we are dealing with infinites and eternals. And since I am receiving, how can I help loving in return? The love that Baba lavishes on each of us cannot but revolutionize us. Spinoza puts it this way: "Minds, nevertheless, are not conquered by force of arms but by love and generosity." Love, like light (truth), reveals itself in the darkness. A lantern may light up a cave that has been dark for ages: no matter how long I've been negative or to what extent, love will carry all before it. I realize that I am using a good deal of rhetoric but I am also desperately trying to grasp that which passeth understanding, and with which I am daily now face to face. That is Baba and His love.

The other day we went to Baba's home at Pimpalgaon, a most peaceful, Biblical area, with small mountains enclosing the valley in which are Baba's buildings and gardens, beautifully kept by the girls. He led us on a hike up the hill where He spent many months in seclusion. There is a holy atmosphere there, and we enjoyed the experience. Baba threw me a little rock, to keep. He showed us around His quarters and where the others stayed. The men sleep mostly on the floor. The women, Rano and Dr. Goher, are in the house. Baba had spent the *Man-O-Nash* period on the mountain — when He worked extremely hard, was exhausted, and wanted "to step out of the Universe." I think the ashram is called "Meherazad" (free, flourishing).* Gustadji, an old disciple, has spent 27 years in silence. An incident was told of Baba saving him from a bath or worse whenihe was on watch and tried to step off into a reservoir in the dark. Baba clapped His hands every time he tried to go forward.

Tuesday, 21st. The news is way ahead of me! Baba will give me a brooch made with His hair for you, He reminded me today.

We were in Sakori yesterday. A great experience. We passed Rahuri Ashram, now disbanded, for *masts* and God-mad. We were supposed to go to Sai Baba's place at Shirdi, but time got there first. We were feasted and dined by Godavri Mai, the woman in charge of the Sakori Ashram. Baba told us a fantastic story of what happened to Upasni Maharaj, but I shall have to tell you in person. It was a beautiful ride of 56 miles each way. On the road we stopped at a well from which water is drawn by eight oxen that go and stop to songs. Otherwise they get too lazy. A band of the ubiquitous gypsies, buffalo cows, camels, baby donkeys, kid goats, calves, colts, women with burdens on their heads, an endless parade of picturesque India. I told Fred W. that *Life* magazine could find plenty of material. Everything is green, although this is semi-desert. Heads must be covered, I found out from a headache.

Played ping pong with Philippe at 5:30 a.m. Baba plays, too. Today He showed us how to play marbles. He offered a prize — but did not give me a marble till the end. I said nothing, because I knew He was doing it on purpose. I discovered, by Baba pointing it out to me, that I am quite assertive. But Baba forgives and we understand each other. The least smell of intellectualism, which for Him is synonymous with hypocrisy, "bothers" Him. He told me to balance mind and heart, with heart having precedence. It is a wonderful lesson, especially having Baba's own example of awakening rather than teaching.

*See page 28

In talking to Malcolm, he mentioned that distractions (of *sanskaras*) clutter up the mind so we can't get at the subconscious, to recall essential things. On the way to Sakori, Baba was very considerate, warning of dust, etc. He put on a scarf, but I said it was dangerous when riding, as it would catch on something. He immediately removed it, no doubt to show me how to be obedient.

Jokes were in order. I told two. A boy was asked by his teacher to define space. "I've got it in my mind," he said, "but I can't think of it." And: A child was asked to define Ireland and answered: "Ireland is like purgatory, a place where people suffer for a while before they go to America."

I'm bringing back pebbles from Baba's ashrams, as He says they have His vibrations. The Sakori Ashram is where Baba lived with Upasni Maharaj for seven years. It was He who gave Baba the Divine Knowledge. It has a wonderful atmosphere. Nuns live there; they speak Sanskrit, as Maharaj was a great scholar.

For the last three nights Baba hasn't slept because of His Work. However, later He said He felt better. John Bass is down with stomach trouble, and I have an ache, too — not used to so much food, or picked up a germ.

Baba asked us to try to see His face in the silence period. I thought of His face and what it expresses:

A line of mastery,
A line of suffering,
A line of joy,
A line of patience.
Between the lines,
The light of His Smile,
The love of His Heart,
The mystery of His Being,
The triumph of His Divinity.

September 12th, 1954 will always stir a profound emotion

in my heart. It was my first *darshan* of the Beloved Master. On the voyage to India I had the good fortune to meet Pratap Madhani, a devotee of Shri Ramakrishna, who had Baba's darshan in New York, in 1952. He referred to Baba as "a very, very great saint" and treasured every word of Baba's message to him at the time as "a priceless pearl." When I introduced myself to him as a Baba-lover on the way to see Him, Mr. Madhani kindly suggested that I repeat the sound 'Om' for ten minutes before each meal, strictly avoid contact with the opposite sex, and become a vegetarian — to purify and raise my vibrations on the holy pilgrimage. Eventually I did all these things, plus a bit of fasting and silence. I did not touch alcoholic beverages during the three months' round trip. We had many inspiring conversations aboard ship, and he delighted me by singing *bhajans**, incidentally, a very effective medium for giving the feeling of God. Later, we were joined by Fred Marks from England, who helped me to realize deeply that Baba is the Avatar of this age, *Paramatman* become human, in His infinite mercy and love for humanity.

So it was with great expectation and eagerness that I awaited my first glimpse *(darshan)* of Baba, that historic morning of September 12th at Ahmednagar. The Westerners squatted on the platform back of where Baba was to sit, facing the huge crowd of Indians under the long, rectangular canopy. The weather was hot but not humid. I wondered how Baba would appear, how He looked, what He would wear, what I would feel. Would He notice me? No, how could He with all that was going on? And yet He did see me, giving me a look of recognition from eyes full of love and compassion, so that I cried.

I was glad we had all dressed our best, as we were near the dignitaries who came to give speeches and *namaskars* to Baba. There was a holy atmosphere; everyone was serious;

*Devotional songs

no begging or bothering of us, as was the case in Bombay. People kept arriving in an endless stream: in the afternoon, waves of shouting schoolchildren swelled the tide, harassing the police and Baba's workers. Some came possibly out of curiosity but the whole populace of Ahmednagar, 85,000, seemed to be present. Many thousands had arrived hours before 9 a.m., the time scheduled for Baba's arrival.

Suddenly, Baba appears. He is dressed in sparkling white clothes, which later were drenched in perspiration from the tremendous labor of handing out *prasad*. Shouts of *"Avatar Meher Baba ki jai!"* greet Him as He quickly walks to His place, surrounded by men Mandali. Most of the *darshan* I had of Baba that day was of His back and the side of His face, but even so I was deeply touched by His power, humility and selflessness. There was hardly a dry eye among those close to Him. Even Sarosh, a businessman and politician, finally pulled out a handkerchief to dry his tears. The idea of *darshan* was so new to me that I, no doubt, missed many points of significance. I could not connect it with any experience I had in the West. Nevertheless, it was quite clear that Baba's Presence aroused the emotions of enthusiasm, fervor, devotion and love in the multitude. It became clear, also, that Baba wants joyful, not sad people. They were happy to get Baba's *prasad*, the gift of God. Although Baba smiled much of the time, we felt He was going through a crucifixion, at least physically. There is always a challenge in the Master's Presence to share His labors, to be loyal, serious and silent. But this was His day; we merely looked on helplessly.

I could not help wondering what effective medium of publicity had been used to get such a big turnout. I forgot to inquire, but the only equivalent in the West to Baba's Mass Darshan would be a troupe of Hollywood stars giving away washing machines and refrigerators as *prasad!* Indians know that with the Master's *prasad* go His blessings and grace, which they value above all things.

In giving the sugar-coated peanuts, Baba held the hand of the recipient and looked into his eyes — the Master's touch, look and word are His usual techniques for affecting a change in people through His high vibrations and pure consciousness. (On the return voyage I invited a young Indian, Mr. Mejerji — meaning 'monkey' — to our Baba meeting aboard ship. He came reluctantly because he said a Master can change you into anything. Also, he did not want his *bhava* — path of natural tendencies — changed.) The touch of the Master is dynamic — you receive by accepting the gift; His eye is the seed for awakening of consciousness; His speech is the most powerful contact. No wonder the people scrambled for His *prasad*. It was a real feast and holy day for the Indians who came from far and near in bullock carts, bicycles and via modern transport. Indians take God in the person of Baba for granted, as we accept the existence of the impersonal God. When Baba left for a short time to feed the thousands of poor, I heard a youth shout "Make way for God" without batting an eyelash. I have found this to be a good *mantra* to recall, symbolically, because, as Baba has said, there are too many beloveds in the house of our life for the One Beloved to enter.

I asked a small boy why he came. He gave me a one-word answer: *"prasad."* An older boy shook hands and said to me: "On this auspicious day you become my bosom friend. This day is very auspicious." Which shows that *darshan* was no mystery to them.

Baba announced to a perfectly silent audience that He would sit for a moment in their midst and then wash the feet of seven old men. Sarosh, the M.C., read Baba's message of the day in which He explained why He does not speak; that "To love God in the most practical way is to love our fellow beings... Spare no pains to help others." When Baba explained the nature of true humility, the people smiled and rolled their heads, a sign of approval in India.

Baba's love, His Presence and wisdom was the answer to their hearts' desire. They were happy, expressing their emotion in concerted shouts of *"Avatar Meher Baba ki jai!"*

Sarosh said that people from all over the world had come to Baba's Last Darshan (from the "four corners of the earth," as the Bible predicted). He introduced the Mayor of Ahmednagar, a very tall, handsome former wrestler, who first garlanded Baba and bowed to His feet. We were given printed translations of his speech,* wherein he acknowledged the tangible and spiritual services of Baba to the district for many years and expressed the people's gratitude, and how honored they felt to have the Avatar in their midst.

I could not understand the speeches of the political figures, as they were probably in Marathi. A Swami, with shaven head and ochre robe, holding some flowers, gave his message, then went and bowed to Baba who passed His hands over his head and face a number of times, affectionately.

A disciple recited by heart what might have been a long poem. I saw Baba wave to someone at the periphery of the crowd, a picturesque *mast* (or saint) with a beautiful face and white, patriarchal beard. He carried a staff and wore a framed picture of Baba. Another speech, more flowers.

As I looked at the sea of faces full of devotion and eagerness to receive the atmosphere of the God-man, I thought I could see in them signs of awakening to the New Life that the Avatar brings. Baba was returning to each one present his own love, transmuted into a divine power that was felt by all. Were they not partaking of the highest yoga — bhakti yoga — the yoga of union? To witness this interplay of human and divine love was to carry away an everlasting experience "not of this world;" Truth in action.

*See page 15

The women and children were first to receive Baba's *prasad*. There was no delegation of work to assistants, Baba personally gave out many thousands of handfuls of sweetmeats, which were in huge baskets. They brought flowers and fruits to the God-man. When a child was pushed away without His *prasad*, Baba would recall him despite the rush. A Brahmin lady tried to garland Baba but He did not permit it, no doubt for her own good. It was very touching to see the joy and adoration elicited from these simple people by Baba. "Baba has chosen well to give His *darshan* to the Indian people," I thought. "The souls of the sophisticated are too veiled to perceive Divinity."

The men, who had been squatting for hours, became restless and noisy, so that there was a near riot by noon. Baba stopped giving *prasad* and a message from Him was given over the microphone. Then the *prasad* for the men was begun. To avoid a rush, they had to crawl under a stick held by the police, who, incidentally took advantage of their proximity to get His *darshan* as often as possible. Sarosh and other disciples kept them moving on with "*Chelo, chelo*" which means 'move on.' Later in the afternoon, the surging crowd again got out of hand. Baba controlled them by standing on His chair for a moment — the remarkable expression on His face has been recorded for us by someone who snapped His picture. Otherwise the mob would have to be controlled with force. As it was, many of them smiled afterwards.

At one point, Baba suddenly left the pavilion and was followed by many of the crowd to where thousands of the poor waited for Him to sit in their midst, a signal for them to be fed with porridge on an improvised plate of natural leaves stapled together, and a beverage. I thought to myself that only a well-endowed organization would undertake such a mission in the West. Here were things being done unselfishly, quietly and efficiently. This was no publicity stunt: the fact is that the *motive* is new in Baba! It is Baba's Love!

With all the tumult, Baba was concerned over the older members of the Western party and called for Will Backett and Charles Purdom, to greet them. Baba also did His universal work, as evidenced by the motion of His fingers, mysterious actions to me until it was explained. At first I mistook it for nervousness. Fred Marks held a cushion at Baba's back. Papa, father of Eruch (the interpreter), and one of Baba's old Mandali, kept wiping the perspiration from Baba's head very lovingly.

To Baba's right, on the platform, were women Mandali pulled out of seclusion, symbolically, as was done by Shri Krishna: The girls wore white saris with a wide, blue border. To Baba's left were two music bands, one being composed of young, middle-aged and older people of both sexes. I watched them as I listened to their strange chanting and bells, and it occurred to me that Baba was using the feminine principle here as a pattern for the future, in the immense subconscious. They performed with fervor and appeared to be lost in the spirit of the dawn of a New Age.

When things became very noisy, a Mandali would shout repeatedly *"Shandra-ha"* which means 'be quiet.' Every so often we had audience participation with cheers of *"Avatar Meher Baba ki jai,"* an impression that is unforgettable.

Late in the day, Baba's right hand gave out, and He continued giving *prasad* with His left. One *had* to be superhuman to withstand all that!

Around Baba were Eruch, Gustadji (the silent Mandali), Adi, Kaka, Krishnaji, Meherji, Sadha (a favorite student of Upasni Maharaj), Viloo, Godavri Mai and an elderly woman. We Westerners got as close as we could. A turbaned old man sat among the crowd in front of Baba, never lowering his *namaskar* to the Master. The saint Gadejai Maharaj, stayed close to Baba all through the *darshan,* except for a while when he harangued a group back of the pavilion. I thought at the time that perhaps he was trying to give Baba some competition, but soon I learned who he was. He seemed immensely impressed, as no doubt he was, because the next day he invited Baba to give His darshan at Pandharpur where several hundred thousand pilgrims come annually to worship Krishna in the form of the statue 'Vithoba,' so named by Sadguru Tukaram. He was overjoyed at Baba's acceptance, as he is very dear to Baba.

It was a unique privilege to have witnessed Baba's Mass Darshan, and feel the strong, invisible bond between the Avatar and His people. He could have told them what He said to me, in my first private interview with Him: "My love brought you here." To them Baba is another Krishna come; He personifies the teachings of the Bhagavad Gita — the incarnation of truth, goodness, compassion, purity, love and oneness. No wonder, then, that He claims their allegiance and calls forth their noblest self in longing to come closer to the Beloved One. As is written in the Gita: "Giving the self in love to Me, with Me as Goal, doing all actions for Me, devoid of all attachment to the forms, free from hostility to any being, man comes to Me...."

II

Reflecting on the September 12th Mass Darshan at Ahmednagar, where I saw Meher Baba for the first time, I thought: this initial, impersonal introduction effectively conveyed to me the feeling that there is much more to Baba than meets the eye. The explosive release of pent-up devotional emotion (reverence, love, longing) on the part of thousands and thousands of those who came for Baba's *darshan-prasad* was clear proof that they were not seeing a mere mortal or eating just sugar-coated peanuts. Incidentally, this 'gift of God' is significant for our lives — a mixture of peanuts and the Avatar's divine love: we must experience ordinary life but be open to His blessings and grace that go with it. Behind the idea of the

Master's *darshan*, feeling the unity of the Self in all selves as a means of transforming the individual recipient and the whole of humanity, are thousands of years of cultural influences — the spiritual leadership of sages, seers, saints, Avatars; scriptures like the Upanishads, the Bhagavad Gita, and the Mahabharata; mysticism expressed through the arts — which have brought to the Indian people the conviction that to behold a pure soul is to be purified, and that the touch, eye and word of the Perfect Master take away *sanskaras*, thus constituting a short-cut to God. Baba is simplicity itself, in His dress and manner: He pierces through the hard crust of sophistication and intellect, speaking to the heart and soul. He opens an inner window in those that come to Him, so that rays of His light, bliss, power and wisdom penetrate our gross-consciousness — and we feel His presence, holiness, purity and love.... the transcendent Baba and His transcendent mission.

Two days later, I had the rare privilege of being introduced to, and embraced by, Baba at the Meherabad Hill ashram where the group of Westerners were His guests. Everyone was somewhat stand-offish at first, still so under the impression of the Impersonal Baba we could not help but feel at the Mass Darshan. The physical proximity of an Avatar was an awesome experience, apparently even for those who have known Him these past twenty-five years, and whom He had already greeted at the Darshan. I thought Baba might take offense at this cool reception, but He broke the ice by saying: "Don't be afraid. Gather round Me like friends." That did it — we were like children of the Merciful Father. We were all smiles and, after the embrace, really warmed up to Him. Baba, with the psychology of the adult who does not wish to spoil the child with overindulgence, told us: this would be the only time He could embrace us, giving the excuse that His heart could not take it — like the multimillionaire telling his youngsters he can't afford to get them a car, for their own good.

The following day, Baba offered a five-minute interview to each of us individually. I was overjoyed "at the opportunity of many life-times," as I had expressed it in the cable asking permission to come to see Baba in India, to come so close to the Source of Light. On the other hand, I felt a tinge of disappointment that "it was only five minutes!" forgetting that "with God, a thousand years are as a day," *i.e.* with Baba one is outside of time, space and illusion, experiencing something of Reality or Eternity (as quality). So to budget my precious time, I wrote out six questions. I wonder now if it did not amuse Baba to see me glance at my notes before speaking each time. One question was: "What is the nature of service in Baba?" Baba appeared to relish that one, because it showed that I realized that loving God is not "a joke" as He said, and quoted the Sanskrit from the *Bhagavad Gita:*
"I want your body, mind and possessions."
I still don't know how long the interview lasted, but I felt I had received bountifully and wrote everything down, so that none of the precious 'jewels' would be lost. In fact, five minutes went by while Baba waited for an individual He had sent for, to introduce me for a second time. Said individual apparently astonished and amused Baba, in answer to His query as to the cause of the delay, by admitting that he was napping upstairs! When he had answered Baba's question as to who I was, Baba again signaled: "So you were sleeping? Do you feel well? All right, go back to sleep!" That's tolerance! The first question Baba asked me was: "Have you met Me before?" I said: "No, Baba." "You have, but you don't remember. You have known Me always," Baba assured me. Next time, God willing, I get Baba's darshan, I shall answer correctly.
As I look over the notes of my Great Odyssey to the Beloved, I see that He wanted us to distinguish between the *darshan* of Baba as man and His *darshan* as God, saying, "Only the pure in heart can see God." "I am one with you on every level, but you know this only when the ego

and intellect do not interfere. Then Baba appears as He is."
"One has to die to oneself to know Me." He asked us to try
to imagine Him in silent contemplation while we were still
there with Baba: "Do it so wholeheartedly that I must feel
it here (pointing to His heart)." "He (God) is not visible,
because he is infinitely visible to that eye which has no veil
of desires, or of ego, over it." The youth who wanted
desperately to see God, and came to Emperor Janak, a
Perfect Master, finally succeeded through proper identity.
Baba explains this "...unless you lose the 'I', you cannot see
and become God, because where you are, God is not." Baba
said that if the Japanese youth, K. Hitaker, would fast in
silence for a week "I may give him just a tiny glimpse of
Me."

At my first private interview with Baba, at Meherabad
Hill Ashram, I showed Him a bound volume of *The Awakener*
(thinking that here I was face to face with the living
Awakener in person!) which had been presented to me by
my friends of the New York Meher Baba Group, on my
departure by boat to India. Since I had not met Baba
previous to answering His Call to lovers in the West to
come for His Last Darshan, I used the inscription over my
friends' signature as a credential to establish me with Him.
He looked surprised but did not attempt to read it, handing
it to Eruch, the interpreter (my turn to be surprised), who
read: "....be our channel of love to Baba as He will make you
a channel of love to the world." Baba smiled and fondled
the book. The interview over, I still was worldly enough to
expect the return of my book. But no, Baba dismissed me
with the volume lying beside Him. "How odd of God to be
absent-minded or misunderstand that I had given it to
Him," I thought to myself.

Shortly afterwards a wind came up and I went diffi-
dently into the lounge where Baba was alone at the
moment, making a sign that I wanted to get my sweater
from the desk drawer where I kept it handy. Baba motioned for me to come to His couch, handing me the

book. In reaching for it, my glasses fell to the floor from my shirt pocket. I stooped down to Baba's feet — something I had wanted to do before but didn't, I suppose, because I felt such an attitude was more of the spirit than a mere overt act — a typical Western inhibition, and in rising kissed Baba's right-hand thumb, as he handed me the book.

Another time, when Baba arrived for one of His discourses to the Western men, He got up from the couch and motioned for me to go out with Him. I was fearful that I had been too much for Him — disobedience, garrulity, what-not? — and that I was next to leave after Max Haefliger, having overstayed my welcome. I was mistaken. In the course of the first interview, I had mentioned that one of our girls wanted a brooch made of His hair (she had lost one). Baba nodded. Several days later, He told me He would bring it the next day. He did, and that is why I was called out (Baba knew my predeliction for drama) — calling me to His couch during a meeting and making me sit beside Him while He showed me a photo; going to the end of the lounge to embrace me first; throwing me a little box which I was to throw back to Him; and later at the top of the Tembe hill where Baba experienced His Man-o-nash, throwing me a little rock to keep; asking me to send Him a certain recording after I had offered another one — always in front of the others. Some preferred a secret relationship with Baba — like Fred Marks, into whose lap Baba inadvertantly threw a flower after he had secretly spread out a rug on Baba's couch. Baba explained to me with signs that the beautiful brooch was made with His hair and finger-nails. As He handed it to me in a box, I kissed His right-hand thumb.

On the following day, when Baba was going down the hill after He had been with us all morning, Fred Marks and I followed. Baba turned and motioned for us to go back, as apparently we had disobeyed an order. We stopped and hesitated to turn back without touching Him. Although He signaled for us to come to Him, I realized that I had not practiced obedience which Baba again and again tried to show me (obedience being next to love ensuring that one is doing Baba's will and not his own). As Baba gave me His hand to shake, I did not feel the thumb, which precluded my trying to kiss it. I am still wondering if there is any connection between this incident and our missing Baba the next morning when He made a surprise visit to the ashram (Fred and I had gone for an exploratory walk lured by the idyllic scenery). On this visit Baba gave out photos of Himself with His signature, and left His final message to us: "To all you meet and see, give My Love — the only thing worth receiving." This message, delivered to me together with Baba's signed photo and a kiss by proxy (Phillipe DuPuis), marks a milestone in my life because shortly afterwards (it 'happened' on the streets of London) I began to love all people I met, instead of being repelled by them.

So, although I had displeased Baba again and again (it being inevitable, since I was a newcomer) and although Baba knew all my faults from the moment He met me, He assured me with words and deeds that "My love will help you." Baba does not work with the negative but from the creative center of the individual himself — which is love.

Why I was given the thumb of the Beloved One's right hand to kiss each time, is anyone's conjecture. It was not accidental, of that I am certain. After the Last Meeting, when Baba called the Western group to give them His prasad of oranges and the last embrace, I did not realize it was the last time I should see Him, and hurried past, as I knew what a terrific strain the last two days were on Him — Baba, looking at me with eyes that would melt a heart of stone, held out His right-hand thumb for me to kiss.

From Philippe Dupuis:

...The main teaching I got from India...was...that spiritual life is no fun, no adventure, no part-time, not excitement! It is like the modern wars. It is total! It is not to be thought only, but lived. The best way to do it is to give up everything — forget everything; be ready and glad to die at the feet of one's Master, if you have the grace to have one. All else seems to me loss of time, compromise. No one can barter with God. This is why I wish I were dead in India, not only to myself but to my body...if B. asked me to do so. To try to be spiritual in the West seems to me to be a mockery. Nothing is in favor of it — even though one would be a hero, a saint, or a giant of strength. To be spiritual we have to go back to school, to India, very humbly, and learn from the presence of our Master. There is nothing like the physical presence of a Master. We have to be ready to give up everything for the Beloved... and die. This poor mind of ours is the main obstacle. It seems only the Master can put it aside for us and unlock our heart — which is the secret of all secrets....Let's go back to school, to the Master! He is our only way, our only hope ... all depends on His Grace. Without Him... darkness on top of darkness. And all the books in the world cannot give one-millionth of the bliss that one look of the Master can bestow on you. The trouble is that to follow a Master you must be a real hero... have a terrific strength which only He can give you. All along, it is a matter of Grace...

He seemed enormously amused to think that we only saw Him for one minute and then Bang! got caught!... He said we were very lucky to be able to recognize an Avatar in such a short time....Another time He said: "There are 99 per cent chances that I shall drop My body before the end of next December. If I would not drop it, I would live up to 90 years of age — sitting on top of the chest of the whole universe."

From Darwin Shaw:

For each of us who had never before witnessed Baba at work with such a multitude, the day of His Last Mass

Darshan was an amazing experience. The interest the Indian people show in a Spiritual Master is, in itself, an example which the people of the West would do well to consider and emulate. Although many of those who attended the Mass Darshan were from Ahmednagar, where the program was held, there were thousands of others who had to travel several miles, either afoot or in bullock carts. Others of Baba's devotees had come from as far as Bombay and Andhra; while we Westerners had, of course, come many thousands of miles.

The Indian people, dressed as they were, in many-hued *saris* and turbans, made a very colorful assemblage. They were from every class and creed. Among them were the aged, the lame and the blind. Many women carried babes in arms. In this huge crowd one felt that the differences, which ordinarily separate one group of people from another, were completely forgotten. We watched as Mohammedans, Hindus, Parsees and Christians commingled with those of so-called higher caste and lower caste, the well-to-do and the very poor, to become one homogenous stream of humanity, united and humble in their appreciation of the great and rare privilege it was for them all to have a personal contact with the God-man. Baba, Himself, declared the importance of this personal contact when He said, "No explanations or discourses can compare with the personal contact. I feel I am in all. It is Baba bowing down to Baba."

Baba made this statement at the so-called "Little Darshan" on September 26th, which was given for those, who, because of the huge crowd on the 12th of September, were unable to contact Him on that day. At this "Little Darshan" about 8,000 people filed past Him — touching His hands or His feet, or placing sweet-smelling garlands of jasmine around His neck. Baba said, "Whatever anyone takes Me for, I am that."

On both days we were near Baba most of the time, and we watched with heartfelt wonder as this profoundly impressive drama between the Divine Beloved and the humanity for whom He has taken incarnation, took place before us. We deeply felt the soul-stirring significance of these long hours of Divine Love in action and, in our hearts, we knew that new Light was being shed along the pathway that humanity must tread on its pilgrimage toward the Infinite.

From Fred Frey Jr.:

On September 19th, 1954, Baba played for us Indian and Persian recordings. In His presence the music itself sounded enchanting, but a sudden thought struck me, "Would this music sound as beautiful when He was not in the same room?" That evening I played the same discs again and they sounded flat. Could it be that my love for Baba was not deep enough to prove that He was and always will be ever present? Without this knowledge, life would be unbearable.

On the following day when He asked me how I had enjoyed the records, I must have sounded unenthusiastic. A quick twinkle was shot my way. From this and the vibrant twitchings of the fingers of His right hand and the expression on His face, I knew that "I was in for something."

Almost at once it became poignantly clear that His love and presence are expressed in all sounds of existence. Sandwiched in between rich and busy days, one was startled from time to time to realize that in the calm of night insects held serenades, and the rustling of leaves was their accompaniment; that the pelting "Elephant Rain" and roaring winds expressed symphonic power; that the rattling and clanging of the "iron monster" that took hours on end to get us from Ahmednagar to Bombay was most delightful; that the many sounds of this large city formed melodies of their own, and that the humming drone of the plane from Bombay to New Delhi was most soothing.

While in New Delhi Baba planned that I be in the home of His East Indian devotees, Mr. and Mrs. W.D. Kain. We exchanged thoughts based on the teachings of our Master. The teachings are identical, but the ways of expressing them vary in the East and the West. The deepest discussions were of Baba's Final Declaration. Among Baba's people, as with us in America, each has his own interpretation of this declaration. We left this subject with the joint feeling that "If the Guru dies and the disciple weeps, it means that both have wasted their lives." Also, "If churches, synagogues, and mosques fall, we must carry on His Love within ourselves until His return."

The first Sunday in New Delhi was spent listening to the most beautiful, fascinating, and penetrating *ragas*, executed by lovers of Baba — all untrained but naturally rhythmic voices of men, women and children, tuned in syncopation with native drums, cymbals and harmonium. Through all was a lifting, sacredly haunting oneness of floating melodies of everchanging intensities in scale patterns and tones. The music was a flow of now happy and now solemn repeated words in amalgamated chants. Each song ended on a joyous, uneven, unexpected and broken tempo.

Back in Bombay Alexander Markey was kind enough to arrange to have his assistant, Ramish Prem, play his *vichitra veena* for us. The beauty of this sophisticated and polished music was beyond description. It sounded like frolicking winds whispering in enchanted caves one moment, and like snorting elephants the next. It is part of the rich classical heritage of India.

When in Lebanon, beneath whispering pines and cedars, we heard deep earthy rumblings underground, which prove to be torrents of gurgling, icy waters flowing unexpectedly from dry and barren rocks.

In Cairo, housed on the "Kasad Khuer" anchored on the banks of the Nile, we welcomed night and moonlight. Seated on deck, we heard the faintly rippling waters caught in a current of nightly sounds. Here we felt His presence everywhere — in the frolicking, twinkling lights, deep beneath the cold waters, high in the black space above — penetrating our inner beings, all wrapped in gentle caressing melody.

New York and her jaded clash of unharmonious harmony mingled with the voices of dear ones, on hand to welcome us. Finally landing on our home soil, we were met by the shrill musical laughter of children and the tingling warmth of loving arms. We are home, knowing that His music and love is and always will be ever present, within the reach of all to share.

From Joseph Hamad Harb:

Joyously and somewhat humbly I declare that it was a supreme privilege to be called and be brought by the Perfect Master to His sphere of activity, for the purpose of receiving personal instruction and guidance on the path to God-Realization. Baba's first message to us upon our arrival in India was, "Be happy!" The anxieties of the trip were dispelled and we were happy. That message was oft-repeated and was kept in our consciousness all during the days that followed. Indeed, we were intensely conscious of the atmosphere of all-pervading Love in Baba's ashram.

Those from the Western hemisphere who participated in the Great Darshan on September 12th, 1954, were invited to be present on the platform of the *pandal* with Him to witness Baba lovingly install and instill the spiritual seed in the hearts of those who came to receive His *prasad*, to awaken them to their spiritual mission in life by giving them the fruit or sweets which are the token of the far greater gift — His Blessed, Divine Love — which each received from the Master for their spiritual awakening.

I cannot and I shall not ever forget the first time He embraced me within His loving arms. It was a most unforgettable feeling — so comforting, so peaceful, so delightful that my gratitude for this supreme privilege was of such indescribable feeling that the tears welled up and overflowed with joy and happiness. I loved Him and didn't want to take my arms away from Him, I wanted more and more of His embracing.

Baba is all Divine Love and He loves all. For those who will take His love, He has more opportunity to give them of His love. Those who do not love Him He loves and blesses, but if they will not take His love, they do not give it a chance to be received by them. He does not ask them to accept some dogma, but in the spirit of humility they obey the God in their hearts. Baba gives more as they will take, or accept, or receive more. We limit love — not He!

Baba will go to any extreme of physical exertion to find and awaken those souls with sincere or utmost yearning for God-Realization.

During the twenty days of our stay at the ashram, every day we looked forward to Baba's coming to see us. We were like youngsters waiting for our Father to come home. Our eyes fixed on the road, anxious to see His blue car approaching, we trooped down to the gate to meet Him and watched and watched until His car disappeared from sight. I was so elated by His presence, so inspired and uplifted by His discourses, I couldn't spare a moment away from Him while it was possible to be with Him.

Divine consciousness is ever flowing through Him, but with such delightful simplicity that it would not overwhelm a child, and yet it is beyond the deepest mind to fathom it. We wanted to absorb Him. The vastness of His Divine Mind and love are so scientific, with such intricate laws, and serious and great as He is, yet He couples all this with such humor that it produces joy in the heart and a perfect picture to the mind. The heart becomes the mind's eye to observe the perfect actions of the Perfect Master, which are subtle, silent, and yet so forceful.

A living Avatar is Self-Realized from Unconscious Divinity to Conscious Divinity; functioning in all planes of existence, with all the directness and accuracy in full harmony of Divine Law and Love; manifesting a dynamic force in all His activities; having the power of Eternal Truth. He is a complete blending of God and man states. This is Baba, "The Highest of the High."

The true disciple, being in the presence of the Perfect Master and privileged to witness the perfect living exemplification of His Masterly Perfection, becomes imbued with Divine Love and Wisdom-knowledge, in spite of his human limitations, dispelling all doubts and human frailty of the mind so long as he accepts the Master in his heart. Then and at that instant, the mind becomes illuminated or enlightened with the true feeling and understanding of God's presence, and of one's own true being.

However, when the ego, through the limited mind with its mental equipment, sneaks in to claim the exclusiveness of such wisdom or spiritual understanding through mere intellect by the assertion of its self-esteem, then it plunges itself and all concerned into a state of confusion and illusion.

On the other hand, when the intellectual excellency is used by the spiritual heart and mind, the result becomes most productive in its manifest expression of wisdom-knowledge in all its functions. That becomes the evidence of Infinite, Divine Consciousness of a Great Being that recognizes spiritual freedom and the one Unity in diversity.

When the disciple is alone, away from the Master, and so-called time passes on, the reflection of such abstract thoughts begin to take shape in the process of integration as he lives them actually in his pursuit of action in awakened consciousness. Then it could be said that "There is nothing higher than Truth but true living!" This procedure eventually will lead the disciple to ultimate Reality.

From F.S. Hendricks:

Prayer

*O GOD, all LOVE, all GOOD, all TRUTH, all BEAUTY,
ALL MERCY, JOY and BLISS and PEACE — pour upon all these
souls in Thy Being at this moment in Eternity, Thy great Blessing of
Love, Power, Joy, Bliss and the Grace of Thy Glory in Peace — that
these souls now imprisoned in finite garment, may finish the work
which Thou gavest them to perform, and let Thy Kingdom Come, and
let Thy Will be done on Earth as it is in Heaven....For all these — in
Heart, let Thy "awakening" Be — the One-in-I — ME — the ONE.
     Lovingly dedicated this 30th January, 1955 A.D. to my
Beloved Master, Shri Meher Baba, In Eternity.*

From Bill Le Page:

I met Meher Baba for the first time when I came to India in
September, 1954. When Baba met the Westerners at
Wadia Park on the 12th of September, He looked at each of
us. During one private interview with Baba, I asked Him to
visit Australia. Baba replied, "I am already there." Once,
when Baba was giving a discourse to the Westerners on
Meherabad Hill, His facial expression was so lovely that a
thought flashed in my mind — 'I wish I could go on seeing
Baba.' Just then Baba said, "The discourse is stopped. Just
look at Me for five minutes." Baba did eventually visit
Australia, in 1956; He came and lived in my house in
Sydney.

From Will Backett:

Baba's guests from the West stayed at Meher Retreat
on the hill at Meherabad, the place where for 30 years He
had made spiritual history, which we re-lived with Him as
He showed us about and recalled periods of seclusion in
different places.

The main building inside the compound was originally a disused stone water tank, 40'x20'x15', in which a door and windows were introduced later, becoming afterwards a center for training Baba's women devotees, Eastern and Western, in strict seclusion.

In the very early period, Baba used to descend alone into the dark depths of the tank for seclusion, which He also did in a cavity outside the compound, which was later roofed over with a dome and will be the tomb for His body when He lays it down. At each of the four corners of the domed roof is a symbol of a great world religion — a cross for Christianity, a crescent for Mohammedanism, a flame for Zoroastrianism, and a temple-dome for Hinduism. Baba has come to put new life into each religion. Under the wonderful Indian sky this beautiful snow-white building, bearing the inscription over the door, "Mastery in Servitude," might seem to have descended from Heaven itself to witness the triumph of Divine Love on earth.

Nearby are the tombs of those close to Baba in the East and West, and one reads "In Eternal Memory of Meher Baba's Blessed Parents, who are now merged in Baba's Infinity."

Baba lovingly pointed also to other smaller stones bearing the names of five faithful dogs who had served Him; one, named "Chum," used to keep guard near His door and would not allow even the Mandali to come near.

He also showed us the shed outside the compound which was used as the original *mast* ashram, and the separate room adjoining it, with an interior partition behind which He remained in strict seclusion, out of sight of the Mandali, except for a small opening for His alphabet board on which He conveyed messages. Such was the burden of spiritual travail and consequent physical suffering that His finger often paused from sheer weakness.

On another occasion when showing these buildings afresh, there was a dead sparrow lying on the floor of the tomb, which Baba gently took in His hand, spelling out "lucky sparrow"... for surely the birds and all creation also benefit from the Master's Presence.

In 1938 an upper floor was added to the tank building, with an outside staircase and tower, which commanded a view of the surrounding country. To the north, between two ranges of hills thirteen miles away, the hill of Pimpalgaon is visible. Baba's ashram is at the foot of Meherabad Hill, where we were also taken by Him, and He conducted us first through the men's quarters. There we met several of His old Mandali members, while Baba explained their lives of seclusion, fasting, meditation or strenuous activity. Here, too, is the tiny room where His *mast* work was done — alone — and the meagre floor covering on which He slept. Outside, someone always kept watch at night to answer immediately any summons from within.

Here, too, was the dismantled blue bus, veteran of many thousands of miles touring throughout India with Baba and His party. In this same bus Baba spent part of the "Great Seclusion" of 1949. Nearby is a shed reconstructed from the two smaller ones erected on Pimpalgaon Hill, one on the summit and one on a ledge of the Hill further down. Baba was in seclusion in both of these huts and said that in future years that hill (at Pimpalgaon) would be venerated and become a great place of pilgrimage.

On another day, we followed Baba, a truly inspiring figure in white, up this same hill in brilliant Indian sunshine, He an embodiment of spiritual grace and energy. He sat down three times in deep thought, and often had to stop to allow us to keep near Him; — we two eldest were directed to rest while He took the others to the summit. How fortunate we were, He said, to be there with Him leading the way. Afterwards we visited the women's quarters at Pimpalgaon, and while we were seated around Him on the verandah, He showed us His two greatest spiritual treasures — a very old patched coat which he wore thirty years ago in the "Prem (Love) Ashram" days, and the pair of old, old sandals worn in 1928. This was the year Babajan came to the railroad crossing at Meherabad and the two Masters met, for the last time.

In years to come, Baba said, people will revere that coat and sandals, and find out "what they contain."

While resting there with Him we were all served a refreshing fruit drink, another instance of Baba's thought of our needs.

While at Meherabad, He would sometimes give us fruit, one by one, or Himself serve each plate, as His *prasad;* and once the Indian waiters and Indian staff shared with us like one family. On another occasion, He walked round the table to place both hands on our shoulders, and the gentle firmness of His touch gave deep significance to that simple gesture. There was much laughter when He circumnavigated the long table to find where He could best tickle each one, joining in the fun Himself, for He likes us to be bright and happy always. At the ping pong table provided for our relaxation, He was a doughty opponent, with unique grace and speed. He also showed us a different game of marbles, awarding a prize to the winner and applauding his skill or luck, as part of the deeper game of Divine Love, which is the Master's real sport.

It was, however, a solemn moment, when towards the end of our stay, Baba sent for glasses of fruit drink, and after dismissing His Eastern followers, put His own lips to each glass, after which each of us partook from one glass.

Truly, as one of Baba's absent Western devotees had written, "we are millionaires in Love, through Baba's grace."

As if to emphasize His universal consciousness and Presence at all times, He said, on other occasions:

"I know everything — I cannot help it."

"Just as when we breathe we do not pay attention to our breathing, and in sound sleep it is automatic and our constant companion, still we do not pay attention to it, — so Baba is there *all the time* and *therefore* you don't feel

Him...."

"It is not easy for you to understand that, though I am here with you in this place, I am also everywhere at the same time."

Taking us to the place outside the compound adjoining His tomb, where He used to give spiritual instruction to the boys at His school, Baba showed us where one of them became conscious of "The Master's Universal Divine Form, which the boy also saw in everyone and everything and enjoyed ineffable spiritual bliss."*

Perhaps it was to prepare others that He said, another morning, "I want you, from tomorrow, to think of Me exclusively for half an hour daily, from 9 to 9:30 a.m., for seven days, sitting alone where you will not be disturbed. Close your eyes and just try to bring before your mind's eye Baba's figure.... If thoughts worry you it does not matter. Let them come and go...." This order was rescinded in three days. Again He said later, "I will show you how to become constantly aware of My presence, and thus live with Me consciously."

After a few days, and before the seven days expired, someone reminded Baba of this promise, to which He responded, "When you rise in the morning, think of Me for one second — just for one second — as if you were putting Me on as you put on your coat; again at 12 noon and 5 p.m., just as you might adjust your tie in a second, and finally the same at night, when getting into bed, which makes 4 seconds in all."

Two of us who came to Nasik with the Western group, in 1937, could recall Baba's emphasis then on punctuality, when He fixes definite times in this manner. To interrupt the bustle of Western life four times daily with a brief second's thought of Baba was to be our part in bringing to fruition the love He bestowed on us during

*Described in *Meher Baba Journal*, Vol. I, No. 4, pp. 20-22

these three unforgettable weeks.

Baba related an incident with regard to a lad of 13 which illustrates not only His sufferings when His instructions are not carried out, but also how He works through unexpected happenings following such omissions. He directed that a full flask of coffee should be provided for Him each morning for a whole year while He was in seclusion, and that was to be His only sustenance. But, day by day, the flask arrived only half full at the hands of an "untouchable" lad who carried it up the hill. At the end of the period He asked those responsible for the reason why it arrived half full, but they assured Him the flask was duly filled each day.

Then Baba called the lad and embraced him, counselling him to tell the truth, and heard from his own lips that he had drunk half the coffee, for he was so tired each day climbing up the hill.

Baba then asked us with a smile what word described drinking after another's lips had touched the vessel, and as no one could reply, He gave the answer — prasad; but with such humor that all had to laugh at the unusual situation of the Avatar taking the prasad day by day of an "untouchable," during seclusion for His universal work, instead of the reversal of their relationship, as one might expect.

Another saying during these weeks was "I would suffer millions of deaths to make someone love our Beloved God, Who alone is worthy of real love — our love." The widely different outlook of this lad and that of the other one who realized Baba's Infinite nature, indicates how widely He spreads His net of Love.

As a voice chanted from within our bus speeding through the soft Indian night to Meherabad and Baba:—

"This Love is not easy. It is an Infinite Ocean of Fire, and we have to swim through it."

Baba's Visit to Arangaon Village
September 24, 1954

As we descended the hill with Baba, groups of villagers
could be seen under the trees and near the *Dhuni* fire, ready
to go to their village, Arangaon, with Him.

Baba welcomed us in the Hall and then called an Indian
devotee who, seated before Him on the floor, chanted
fervently about the love for the Divine Beloved, one of
those age-old sacred songs of India, himself gazing lovingly
in the face of Baba who was bending forward slightly
enrapt in response. Then we followed Him, with our
hearts thus kindled afresh, to the *Dhuni* fire, which He lit,

Adi, Aloba, Meher Baba, Eruch — Aloba saying Muslim prayers at
Dhuni *fire.*

and the perfume and flame of the burning sandalwood rose amidst the cries of *"Avatar Meher Baba ki jai!"* — the deep voices of the Mandali swelling the chorus of the assembled villagers. Primitive music of clashing sticks, drums, bells and horns added a haunting rhythm to the Master's Presence, now seated and garlanded before the *Dhuni*. With that unique grace so natural to Himself, Baba moved forward and lifted onto the raised platform a tiny, naked, shy little boy, caressing him until the little fellow broke out into smiles, reflecting the happiness of all during the whole journey. Soon Baba turned His step toward the village, led by the band and a group of male dancers in two lines facing each other. Leaping from right to left, into each other's place and back again, they skillfully sustained the rhythm while progressing sideways; we who followed could observe, unbroken, two lines of dancers forming and re-forming while they looked sideways at Baba, in whose honor this traditional primitive dance was given.

As the crowd gathered from the village ahead, we could distinguish many roofless walls, with improvised covering and mounds of rubble bordering the narrow, twisting streets where an open gateway sometimes led into a deserted courtyard, giving access to an inner room. Here and there, a narrow passage threaded its way between gloomy walls to yet another one-room home where Baba was welcomed with *arti* and garlands.

Sometimes, the approach was decorated with tiny flags or the pathway bordered with colored chalk patterns, and there were eager faces at doorways to gaze at Baba while the more venturesome bent to pay homage by touching His feet, for He checked no one.

Tethered goats and bullocks, startled by the approaching throng, seemed to turn to gaze at Baba in His progress, and wayward donkeys, with here and there a scurrying, diminutive hen, completed the picture of village life stirred by Baba's advent. Once He did pass by an open doorway and then returned, to enter and find His way through the semi-ruined courtyard into another darkened door, where an old man and his feeble wife and a younger woman were preparing *arti*, which Baba allowed, accepting their gift of a coconut, the symbol of their complete surrender, of body, mind, energy and soul. It was indeed a touching, sacred sight to witness such devotion, and Baba's blessing and Love, as man and wife helped each other to prostrate before Him.

In other homes which we entered with Baba, a garlanded picture of Him and of other Masters decorated the walls of the single room which sometimes lacked a couch, that otherwise seemed to be the sole furniture.

As the door opened, shining brass water vessels, reflecting the light, broke through the darkness, while the eye, now accustomed to the prevailing gloom, could trace the low roof. Women had spread their *saris* on this special occasion on the floor, a pathetic witness to love abounding, awakened by the Grace of the Master and sustained by those united with Him.

Baba also stopped at some of the street corners where special welcomes were prepared in the open. But the crowds pressed so hard upon Him in the narrow, twisting lanes that He had to stop sometimes for us, for He wanted us always near Him, to see the people's daily life. At one crowded spot, He cleared a space and disclosed some grain on the ground, as if recently threshed. It looked like a small millet, the staple food of the people, which the women bring to Meherabad from miles around to have it ground in a mechanical mill Baba has provided at a nominal charge.

Some of the semi-ruined walls and village doorways show ancient artistic design and workmanship side by side with corrugated iron roofing, reflecting the poverty of the inmates, many of whom despite their rags, wore gay *saris* and gay turbans, or white *dhotis* and headdress; and children, like their elders, had necklaces, rings and bangles, for everyone wished to look his best for the occasion.

One saw and felt that Baba is one with them. Has He not declared to us, "I am the poorest of the poor, as I am also the richest of the rich."

As we approached the quarters where the untouchables live, the outcasts of Indian society, Baba spoke of their plight and abject poverty which their homes reveal. He showed us the dwindling pool of water where, when the bed is dry, they dig below the surface for any moisture available. In one home which Baba had had built, lives the cook for Meherabad, who is in Baba's permanent employment there, a standing challenge to the caste system. Thirty years ago, Baba declared, striking His own body before a protesting Brahmin, "I have taken this body that I may destroy the caste system root and branch."

At the entrance to the village, Baba was welcomed at the temple into which we followed Him through the low doorway where men, women and children were gathered. Chairs were provided for the Master and the Mandali and Westerners, who marked the zeal with which all approached Him, including the youngest, and their joy at His loving touch and gracious smile when their turn for *ladhus* (sweets) brought them the Master's hand also. *Darshan* culminated in an excited scramble for bananas which Baba threw singly, here and there, amongst those seated on the floor; His animated face and figure radiated grace, love and happiness as He watched the youngsters vying with each other, unconscious of the spiritual significance of His welcome gifts.

Opposite the entrance to the temple is an alcove for a small-wheeled ritual car which is used once a year and drawn through the streets by eighteen people, with the priest standing erect. As we left the temple, we could see Baba who had mounted the vehicle, seated Himself in full view facing the people. Many would doubtless remember Him there each year as their ceremony recurred.

There was also one other incident in the corporate life of the village when a small group of girls danced and sang in unison on a raised platform, around which chairs had been arranged for Baba and His party.

Baba followed their movements with close interest as the tiny ones danced demurely with the older girls setting the rhythm and pattern, and the large crowd assembled in the open space below could see Him quite clearly. Women massed in gay colors, shoulder to shoulder with their little ones, stood motionless on a raised section of the broad way in front of Baba, the whole of which was packed with people as He gave *ladhus* again to the scores streaming up from below.

Finally, Baba visited the family quarters of one of His Mandali, temporarily occupied by three women members who normally live on the hill, and it was a moving sight to witness their homage and surrender symbolized by a coconut broken at His feet.

He then drove off in His car to the isolated tuberculosis sanitorium half a mile away, to respond to a request for *darshan* there, but He would not allow the Westerners to accompany Him, directing them to the hall where, with His accustomed forethought, He had provided soft drinks. On His return, He shook hands with each of us individually, thus closing an afternoon unique in our experience.

LIST OF BOOKS
BY MEHER BABA

Beams from Meher Baba
Discourses
The Everything and The Nothing
God Speaks
Infinite Intelligence
Life At Its Best
Listen, Humanity
Meher Baba's Tiffin Lectures
The Path of Love

For more information about Meher Baba
visit the Avatar Meher Baba Trust website:
www.avatarmeherbabatrust.org

There are many books about Meher Baba
and various phases of His unique work.

For further information, contact:

IN THE U.S.

Sheriar Foundation
603 Briarwood Drive
Myrtle Beach, SC 29572
www.sheriarbooks.org

Companion Books
www.companionbooks.org

IN INDIA

Meher Book House
email:meherbookhouse@gmail.com
Hyderabad
www.meherbookhouse.com